DEDICATION

To all the people living in the Bo-Kaap, who help to make this 'The Colourful Heart of
Cape Town', and to the memory of those vast numbers plucked from their homelands as
slaves or political prisoners, who made this their 'New Ground'.

Bo-Kaap

Colourful Heart of Cape Town

MICHAEL HUTCHINSON

davidphilip

ACKNOWLEDGMENTS

A book of this nature could only have been made possible with the invaluable input of numerous people connected with or living within the Bo-Kaap, to whom I am truly grateful. Whilst space unfortunately does not permit mention of all, the following people require specific credit:

Shereen Habib proved to be a font of knowledge and insight into the community; your enthusiasm, laughter and scrumptious Malay cooking was truly an inspiration. To Taliep Petersen and Midge Adams, whose talent and collective knowledge gave real insight into the great musical heritage of the Bo-Kaap. Abdeya da Costa, thank you for the many long chats and reminiscence over *samoosas*. Thanks to the family of Achmat Davids who welcomed me into their home and provided much historical background of the area. To all those connected with the mosques and *kramats* who gave information and permitted me to photograph them. To Goosain Emeran who provided an insight into Islamic religious practices. Thank you to Nasser Palangi and Farideh Zariv for permission to include your artwork in the text. To the Ahmed family of Atlas Trading who provided an insight into the spice trade and a selection of traditional recipes from the area. The Jaga family, Armien Allie, Abdullah Osman, Achmat Soni, Ishmael Achmat, Sharifa Fredericks and Faghmie Solomons whose personal stories gave colour to the life of the Bo-Kaap. To Dr MC D'Arcy and Mahmood Sanglay whose knowledge and expert advice proved a highly valuable reference source. Finally, thanks to all those involved with the production of this book, with a special mention to my project manager Cherie Wright who spurred me on to completion and worked well beyond the call of duty.

PHOTOGRAPHIC CREDITS

Photographs throughout the book provided by the author, unless otherwise stated below:
Midge Adams: pp. 92, 94; Abdeya da Costa: pp. 37, 56, 63, 71, 113, 117, 118, 119; Shereen Habib: pp. 3, 9, 38, 60, 67, 73; 87, 93, 97, 124; Deirdré Hewitson, Online Images: pp. 30, 31; Reproduced from the National Archive: pp. 21, 41 (E8677), 45 (M1077), 53 (E9147), 111 (E9048), 112 (E8693), P Lyons Collection, pp 114, 115, 120; Faghmie Solomons: pp 126, 130, 132, 133; Riaz Ismail: p. 104; Trace Images: p. 129.

The Publisher has made every effort to trace and acknowledge copyright holders. In the event that any images have been incorrectly attributed or credited, the Publisher will be pleased to rectify any omissions at the earliest opportunity.

Published in 2006 in southern Africa by David Philip Publishers,
an imprint of New Africa Books (Pty) Ltd,
99 Garfield Road, Claremont 7700, South Africa

© in text Michael Hutchinson 2006
© in published work New Africa Books 2006

ISBN 10-digit: 0-86486-693-3
ISBN 13-digit: 978-0-86486-693-6

Text consultant: Mahmood Sanglay
Project management: Cherie Wright
Editing: Mariëlle Renssen
Proofreading: Sean Fraser
Maps: Bennie Kruger
Cover design: Abdul Amien
Text design and layout: Fresh Identity

Printed and bound in the Republic of South Africa by Pinetown Printers.

Contents

PUBLISHER'S NOTE: There is some variance between sources in the spelling of certain Arabic words; where this is the case, the most common spelling usage has been adopted.

A Tour through the Bo-Kaap

❧❀❧

Bo-Kaap: The Colourful Heart of Cape Town

❧❀❧

For generations we have come
From far-off lands,
Where Malaysian and Indonesian shores
Whisper of our ancient ancestral sands,
Which we perchance could emulate
On this Tana Baru, our 'new ground' …

As artisans we worked to mould
The buildings of the Cape,
Our destiny to fashion,
A new community to make.
Throughout, the call to prayer is heard
From minarets of mosques around …

Though centuries have passed,
Our forebears long since gone,
We stand united
And call as one.
In Bo-Kaap – the Colourful Heart of Cape Town
A new identity we have found …

Dila

A Tour through the Bo-Kaap

For visitors to Cape Town, entering the Bo-Kaap is like stepping into another world. The modern setting of the city centre suddenly changes and you become much more aware of cobbled streets, mosques and brightly coloured houses. A rainbow burst of orange, yellow, pink, blue and green comes into view and stretches up towards Signal Hill. This surreal splash of colour gives the Bo-Kaap a fantastical feel – it's hard to believe that the area was not always this cheerful. During the apartheid era, the National Monuments Council would not permit residents to paint their houses in such a fashion. It was only with the release of Nelson Mandela from prison in 1990 that the colours burst forth – almost as a protest at all those years of oppression!

Today the Bo-Kaap falls between Strand Street, Buitengracht Street, and Carisbrook Street and is made up of the 'Malay Quarter', Stadzicht, Schotsche Kloof and Schoone Kloof. A map of the area with places of interest marked may be found on page 17. The Group Areas Act of 1950 (see page 115) declared the Bo-Kaap for the exclusive use of the Cape 'Malay' Muslim community, however things are changing. The gentrification of the area is a major cause for concern to long-term community members. According to the *Collins English Dictionary*, gentrification is defined as a process by which middle-class people take up residence in a traditionally working-class area of a city, changing the character of the area. By this means deteriorated neighbourhoods experience urban restoration and an increase in property values, along with an influx of wealthier residents. Gentrification can change the demographics of neighbourhoods and may include the displacement of lower-income residents.

Houses in the Bo-Kaap today are highly sought after as investments; prices are soaring and the identity of the area is indeed beginning to alter. It's easy to understand the temptation to capitalise on property prices, as the free-market economy results in a major increase in value. This has had both positive and negative repercussions, and is hotly debated as Shereen Habib, who runs Tana Baru Tours (see page 137), explains:

'We do not mind if people buy and then come to live amongst us, but if they keep buying and selling overnight, the area will lose its identity. There'll be no vibe here anymore ... it'll be silent.'

For the time being, however, the 'vibe' is very much alive. The oldest area of the Bo-Kaap – the Malay Quarter, is now loosely defined by, to the west, Dorp Street, to the north Chiappini Street, Strand Street at the eastern extent, and finally, Buitengracht bounding it to the south. However, this was not always the case. The Bo-Kaap used to reach much further into the city bowl. The exact boundary is hard to classify but it probably extended up from the Company Gardens. As the CBD expanded, so the community was pushed further up Signal Hill.

ORGANISED WALKING TOURS

Shereen Habib was one of the first to set up walking tours of the Bo-Kaap area in 1990. She had been involved with the ANC and the anti-apartheid struggle for many years, and she realised that as well as political action, it was also vitally important to present and maintain a cultural identity. Using her knowledge of the community, she started to give tours to professors and school groups, and as the demand grew, these developed into more organised walking tours aimed at both South African and international visitors to Cape Town and the Bo-Kaap. When she met Nelson Mandela at the International Tourism Indaba held in Durban in 1995, he said to her, 'You are my girl; you have to show off this area to the rest of the world.' Foreign tourists had for many years shunned South Africa, but with the end of apartheid, it was starting to open up once more. The Muslim community is a vital constituent in the make-up of South Africa's new multicultural democracy, which is often referred to as the 'Rainbow Nation'.

When visiting the Malay Quarter, in order to get a sense of the history of slavery, which first brought the ancestors of so many people living here today, it's worth paying a visit to the Slave Lodge. Thereafter you will gain a true feel of the unique nature of the community by strolling through the Bo-Kaap.

Shereen usually begins by taking her tours to the Auwal Mosque (this is also referred to as the Owwal or Owal mosque) – the oldest in South Africa – situated in Dorp Street. Most mosques are happy to receive visitors, but it is advisable to ask the *imam* or caretaker before entering; it's impractical for a non-Muslim to enter during one of the five daily prayer times. Certain protocol should also be respected: shoes need to be removed and ladies should cover their head with a scarf, if possible.

The Auwal Mosque was built in 1798 on property that had been purchased by a freed Muslim slave, Coridon van Ceylon, and it was the first formal centre of worship, education and dissemination of Islamic culture in South Africa. An early history of this and other mosques in the area may be found in Chapter 5.

From the Auwal Mosque, a steep climb up Dorp Street takes you to Cape Town's oldest Dutch house – which stands next to the oldest British house! The houses are privately owned so viewing inside is by special permission only.

Shereen Habib and guests viewing the Bo-Kaap Heritage Mural, Wale Street

The Slave Lodge
(Previously called the South African Cultural History Museum)
Corner Adderley and Wale streets, tel: 021 460 8240
Monday to Friday, 08:30–16:30; Saturday, 09:00–13:00
Closed Sundays, Good Friday and Christmas Day

Slavery was the gateway through which much of Cape Town's Muslim community first set foot on South African soil. The Dutch East India Company (or VOC, which stands for Verenigde Oostindische Compagnie) built the Slave Lodge in 1679, making it the second oldest colonial structure after the Castle (built between 1666 and1679), which is still standing in the Cape today. From 1679 onward, for a period of 31 years, the building housed slaves who belonged to and worked for the Dutch East India Company, as well as convicts and the mentally ill – this amounted to nearly 9000 men, women and children.

In 1810, part of the building was modified to accommodate governmental offices, and the governor, the Earl of Caledon, sold a number of the slaves at a public auction. The following year, the remaining slaves were moved to a rented building; and thereafter, in 1820, to a new slave lodge in the Company Gardens. These 135 slaves were

The main entrance to the Slave Lodge on Adderley Street

released in 1828, six years before the universal emancipation of slaves throughout the British Empire.

Over the years since then, the Slave Lodge in Adderley Street has housed the governor's Advisory Council, the upper house of the first Parliament, the Cape Supreme Court, first library, first post office, Deeds Office, and the Women's Auxiliary Services of the South African Defence Force. Certainly a varied assortment of roles! Then, in the 1960s, it was restored and opened as the South African Cultural History Museum. The building was renamed the Slave Lodge in 1998 and has been amalgamated as part of the Iziko Museums of Cape Town.

Two galleries on the ground floor of the Slave Lodge house a permanent exhibition on slavery, tracing the family roots and ancestry of many of the people living in South Africa today. The exhibition aims to increase awareness of issues such as human rights, equality, peace and justice. It highlights the processes of enslavement and the ship voyages that brought many of the Malay slaves to Cape Town. Newly created exhibition galleries show that the Cape was an integral part of the Indian Ocean slave trade route, with slaves coming from four main areas – Indonesia, India-Ceylon, Mozambique and Madagascar. This contrasts with the route of the transatlantic slave trade, used by European traders to transport African slaves to the plantations of the Americas and the Caribbean. An alcove within the gallery features an interactive column of light that commemorates slaves kept captive at the Lodge. Another room uses sound, projected images and animation to recapture the conditions under which the slaves lived.

The upper galleries (designed by Cape Dutch master architect Michel Louis Thibault) on the Bureau Street side of the Slave Lodge hold a selection of ceramics from South Africa and various parts of the world, including Chinese porcelain from the Tang dynasty (618–907CE). The Silver Gallery displays a range of domestic and commemorative objects of Cape, English, Malaysian and Russian origin.

Moving on from the Slave Lodge, the next cultural destination is the Bo-Kaap Museum, where visitors can orientate themselves to the area and also learn more about Muslim culture.

The Bo-Kaap Museum – one of the oldest houses in the Bo-Kaap

The Bo-Kaap Museum
71 Wale Street, tel: 021 424 3846
Monday to Saturday, 09:30–16:30
Closed Sundays, Eid holidays, Good Friday and 2 January

The museum is located in one of the oldest residential houses of the area. In the 1760s, Jan de Waal started the first housing development in the Bo-Kaap; this house dates to 1768. In fact, it's the only example of Jan de Waal's work that retains its original form. It was first the home of Abubakr Effendi, a well-known Turkish scholar and prominent leader in the Muslim community. He was brought here to help quell feuding between Muslim factions, and is believed to have written one of the first books in the Afrikaans language.

The Bo-Kaap Museum was established in 1978 by Iziko Museums, and gives a unique insight into the cultural history. It acts as the starting point for many of the walking tours of the Bo-Kaap, which provide a wonderful opportunity to get to know the area. (Contact details for official guides are listed at the back of this book.) The museum is furnished to depict the lifestyle of a 19th-century Muslim family. Exhibits tell the story of the local community within a sociopolitical and cultural context.

In the upper exhibition gallery and conference room of the Bo-Kaap Museum, a photographic exhibition by famous Cape photographer George Hallet portrays his impressions of life in the Bo-Kaap. Alongside this, another display highlights the influence of apartheid and laws such as the Group Areas Act on the structure of the community.

Permanent exhibition at the Bo-Kaap Museum

At the time of writing, a temporary travelling exhibition at the museum focused on the artwork of Iranian-Australian artist Farideh Zariv. As she observes, 'There is a warm connection between Persian culture and that found in the Bo-Kaap.' The exhibition, entitled 'The Hand of Fatima', refers to Fatima Zahra, the daughter of the Prophet Muhammad. The original sculpture, the *Hand of Fatima* on which the exhibition is based, holds the unifying influence of the Islamic and Persian culture; it is a symbol of the providence and hospitality of God. Many designs and motifs carry a written verse from the Qur'an – such verses are believed to have protective power.

'The noblest of riches is the abandonment of grasping desire'
Farideh Zariv, mixed media

7

Entrance to the Bo-Kaap Heritage Mural

The Bo-Kaap Heritage Mural
Wale Street
24-hour public access

One of the most exciting recent developments in the area is the Bo-Kaap Heritage Mural designed by international artist Nasser Palangi, husband of Farideh Zariv. Born in 1957 in Hamedan, an Iranian city with a heritage of over 3000 years, Nasser grew up in a family of highly skilled carpet-makers and followed his natural gift in the fine arts sphere. He moved to Tehran when he was young, and continued his fine art studies at Tehran University.

Today a celebrated mural artist residing in Canberra, Australia, Nasser works throughout the world using his paintings to bring healing and harmony to communities. He enlisted the help of a number of local artists within the community to bring his vision to life and a dedication plaque pays tribute to the talents of the artists involved. The mural is painted on the walls of a passageway leading onto Wale Street, and walking through it is like passing into a time capsule. At the entrance, life-sized colour paintings of children, representing the new generation, look on in wonder at a series of monochrome images from the rich history of the area: the first mosque, the *kramat* of Sheikh Yusuf of Macassar, craftsmen, *madrassah* teachers, and the clothes and fashion of a bygone era. The mural illustrates the many positive images of life in the community and celebrates the diversity of culture that we find here in the centre of the city.

Nasser Palangi reflects, 'I was so moved by the generous spirit of the people of the Bo-Kaap that I wanted to give them something in return. I wanted to make it something special, to remind them of their amazing heritage and cultural identity. These are very special people who come from a long tradition of artisans and craftsmen, historians and teachers. I believe that in order to have a clear idea of where we are going, it is important to remember our unique identity and where we have come from. This mural is from the people, with the people, for the people.'

For a more rounded picture of the city's heritage and the influences that moulded its people, visitors may find it worthwhile to visit the District Six Museum at 25A Buitenkant Street (tel: 021 466 7200). District Six was originally established as a mixed community of freed slaves, merchants, artisans, labourers and immigrants, so named in 1867 because it was the sixth municipal district of Cape Town at the time. District Six was a vibrant centre with close links to the city and the port. However, where the Group Areas Act of 1950 to all intents and purposes 'saved' the community of the Bo-Kaap, it destroyed that of District Six. In 1966, it was declared a 'white area' under the Act of 1950; by 1982 the life of the community was over. About 60 000 people were forcibly removed to barren outlying areas aptly known as the Cape Flats, and their houses in District Six were mercilessly flattened by bulldozers.

The mural artists from right, Nasser Palangi, Adenaan Esmael, Mahbod Salahshor, Farhana Randeree, Veronica Wilkinson and Ishmael Achmat.

The Bo-Kaap Heritage Mural illustrates the rich cultural heritage of the early inhabitants of the Bo-Kaap

The Tana Baru

To the uninitiated, the words Tana Baru evoke visions of an exotic location in the Middle East. In fact, Tana Baru, which means 'new ground', refers to the disused Muslim cemetery at the top of Longmarket Street running through the Cape Town city centre. It is composed of three independent burial grounds, lying adjacent to each other and forming a continuous land mass. Two of these burial grounds are on land granted to the Muslim community in 1805 and 1842 respectively; the remaining one comprises private plots. In his book *The History of the Tana Baru*, author Achmat Davids says:

'This piece of land represents the most important Muslim Cemetery in South Africa. Here lie buried the pioneers of Islam in this country … They were the master builders, tailors, masons, dressmakers and labourers who built Cape Town into a functional city.'

The story behind this land offers an interesting and at times confrontational early social history of the community living in the Bo-Kaap. The Tana Baru is most likely the oldest existing Muslim cemetery in South Africa, with some of the earliest records of its use dating back to 1772. Up until 25 July 1804, it had been prohibited to openly practise the religion of Islam at the Cape. On this date, as an expression of goodwill, officials of the Batavian Republic (northwest Java, Indonesia) granted religious freedom to the Cape's Muslims.

With this newfound freedom came two specific privileges: namely, the right of the community to build a mosque, and the granting of an official Muslim burial site. The following year, on 2 October 1805, a portion of the land was given to Frans Of Bengal by the local authorities, for the purpose of Muslim burials. For the community, it assumed a highly significant role as a symbol of their newly acquired religious freedom. It thus became known as the Tana Baru, or 'new ground'. There was always the fear that their privileges would be revoked – but as long as the Tana Baru was in use, the Muslim community could stand firm.

10

Entrance to the Tana Baru on Dawes Street

AFTERMATH OF POVERTY AND LACK OF EDUCATION

During the 19th century, wave after wave of smallpox epidemics hit Cape Town. As early as the smallpox epidemic of 1812, it became evident, though, that the Cape Muslim community was avoiding the officials of the Vaccine Institute, established in 1811 to ensure the vaccination of the entire population. It also came to the officials' notice that those Muslims who *had* been vaccinated would suck one another's arms in an effort to remove the vaccine 'poison'. Obviously, there was a lack of education about the nature of communicable diseases and their prevention, particularly amongst the poorer sector of the society.

Most people living in the Bo-Kaap at that time had just been freed from slavery and their lifestyles were characteristic of any community living in a culture of poverty. Overcrowding, squalor and ignorance were commonplace, and they had every reason to suspect government officials.

The *imams* at the time believed smallpox to be a judgement from *Allah* rather than a communicable infection, so they freely moved between the houses of those infected. Whenever the authorities tried to stop them in the interests of public health, this was seen as interference in their religious practices and the community became defiant. Community members frequently hid their patients and failed to report smallpox cases because the authorities denied Muslim burial rites to those smallpox patients who died in hospital. This angered the devout because in the Muslim faith ceremonial washing of the body, followed by enshroudment prior to burial, is compulsory.

SYMBOL OF RELIGIOUS FREEDOM

With the height of the smallpox epidemic of 1858, problems focusing on the burial grounds in Cape Town started to emerge. In October of that year, the colonial secretary, Rawson W Rawson, wrote a letter to the commissioners of the Municipality of Cape Town, drawing their attention to the 'over-crowdedness, position and condition' of cemeteries within their municipality. For a number of years thereafter a debate raged over the quality of burial grounds and the public health risk they presented, but no definitive action was taken.

Then, in June 1882, smallpox again hit Cape Town, which was caught off guard because there was only a very limited supply of vaccine in the city. In 1883, the Cape Parliament passed a Public Health Act, which laid down conditions for the control of burial grounds, one of which prevented carrying of the dead to the cemetery as this was seen as a means of spreading the disease. The ruling was highly inflammatory since this practice was also considered obligatory within the Muslim faith. Ultimately the Public Health Act directed the closure of the Tana Baru and the Muslim community was instructed to rather bury their dead away from the centre of Cape Town at the cemetery in the outlying suburb of Maitland. The feelings of the community were so strong that public protests began.

When the Tana Baru was officially closed on 15 January 1886, there was great unrest in the Bo-Kaap. Two days later, in an act of open defiance, 3000 Muslims arrived at the Tana Baru to bury a child. The *imam* was arrested but charges were subsequently withdrawn. This dispute over burial rights and grounds led eventually to the formation of the Moslem Cemetery Board.

No burials have taken place at the Tana Baru since 1886, but the land remains a significant site of the Bo-Kaap, acting as a symbol of religious freedom and representing the last resting place of a number of early religious leaders of the community. A new entrance gateway to the Tana Baru has been erected and plans are in place to rejuvenate the land and create a garden of peace and remembrance.

KRAMATS OF THE TANA BARU

Three *kramats* have been erected to prominent early Cape Muslim *imams* who lie buried on the Tana Baru. The word *kramat* literally means 'saint', 'wonder' or 'miracle' in Arabic but in this country it generally refers to a holy shrine where one of the saints of Islam has been interred. In the Muslim tradition these revered *imams* are referred to using the term 'Tuan' (meaning 'Sir' or 'Mr' in Arabic) as a sign of respect.

Tuan Guru

Imam Abdullah *Kadi* Abdus Salaam, best known as Tuan Guru, was a prince from Tidore in the Ternate Islands (Indonesia) and was brought to the Cape in 1780 for conspiring with the English against the Dutch. While imprisoned on Robben Island, Imam Abdullah wrote a book on Islamic jurisprudence and several copies of the Holy Qur'an (Koran) from memory. His handwritten works became the main reference work for 19th-century Cape Muslims and had a tremendous influence on Islam in the Cape. Upon release from the island in 1793, he

established the Dorp Street *madrassah* (also *madressa*), which was the first organised school where the Qur'an was taught to slaves and free black children. Hence Imam Abdullah's nickname Tuan Guru, meaning 'Mister Teacher'. This *madrassah* was the first of its kind in the Cape; by 1832, 12 such schools were operational. Tuan Guru was also highly influential in the opening of the Auwal Mosque in Dorp Street. His shrine looks like a partially collapsed pyramid and has palm trees growing beside it. A plaque at the shrine commemorates the route of Tuan Guru's exile from Indonesia in 1780.

Pyramid structure of the kramat *to Tuan Guru with a view (above) of the grave inside*

Tuan Sayeed Alawse

When Tuan Sayeed Alawse of Mocca, Yemen, in southwest Arabia, arrived in the Cape in 1744, he was classified as a *Mohammedaansche priester*, and was sentenced to 12 years in prison. Whilst captive he spent much of his time teaching the other prisoners about Islam. Upon his release he forgave his jailer and became a policeman, which allowed him free access to work with the prisoners. Legend tells of how he used to secretly enter the guarded slave quarters at night to teach them from the Qur'an and later return with food. The guards could never explain how he managed to pass them unawares. When he died in 1803 he was buried under a simple tombstone of Robben Island slate. This has now been replaced with the unusual design of the *kramat*, which may be visited in the Tana Baru today.

The kramat *of Tuan Sayeed Alawse, which looks out over Table Bay*

Tuan Nuruman

Higher up the hill in the Tana Baru stands the shrine to Tuan Nuruman, or Imam Norman, who was elected as *imam* of his people while he resided in the Slave Lodge. He was the only *wali* known to have been a slave. *Wali* is an Arabic word, meaning 'protector' or 'guardian'. In the Islamic tradition a *wali* or *WaliAllah* is a friend of God who has direct access and acts as an oracle. From the time he arrived in Cape Town in 1779, Tuan Nuruman was considered a prophet as a result of the good deeds he performed. People said that a light or aura emanated from his body when he prayed. In 1786, he was sent to Robben Island for his involvement in a planned escape bid from the Slave Lodge. Upon his release, he settled among the free black people in the city and, at the age of 80, he was still working at repairing the roads of Cape Town. When he died in 1810, he was buried on the plot of land within the Tana Baru that had been given to him by General Janssens, commander of the Cape, as a token of friendship. In contrast to the others, his *kramat* is a very simple structure – a tombstone atop a mound of rocks.

The Noon Gun Tea Room & Restaurant
273 Longmarket Street, tel: 021 424 0529
Open weekdays 10:00–22:00 except during Ramadan*, when it is open lunchtimes only*

No tour of the Bo-Kaap would be complete without a sample of authentic local cuisine. The Noon Gun Tea Room at the top of Longmarket Street affords one of the best views of the city bowl, mountain and Table Bay. Be warned it is a steep climb to the top, and not for the faint-hearted! The Tea Room is named after the famous booming timekeeper on the hill. The owner, Mariam Misbach (Shereen Habib's mother) is one of the great characters of the area. She recalls with a chuckle how, at the top of this street, the brakes of her husband Anwar's car failed a few years ago as he set off for the family greengrocers. He hurtled off down the street before veering off onto the verge. 'Since then he has checked the brake fluid regularly!' she laughs.

Her house is a Bo-Kaap landmark and has stood looking out across the city for over 150 years. Mariam and her family have lived here for more than 50 of those years. At the age of 13, she moved here from Hanover Street in District Six, after her parents bought it from a Portuguese immigrant at the end of World War II.

The Tea Room is a family-run affair with herself, her children and grandchildren taking turns in the kitchen and serving patrons. They offer traditional Malay cuisine and the menu consists of a fixed three-course meal, which alters each day. (Those with dietary preferences should specify this when booking.) Tea, coffee and fruit juices are served throughout the day; in line with Muslim custom, alcohol is not permitted.

View of the Tea Room, looking towards Table Mountain

The Noon Gun, Lion Battery
Follow the signposts from Buitengracht Street to the top of Military Street

The best time for a visit is just before midday, to witness the daily firing of the noon gun – Cape Town's oldest and most enduring tradition. The two guns used are also the oldest in daily use in the world. In 1795, shortly after the English occupation of the Cape, the Dutch guns installed at the Castle were removed and replaced by the latest English 18-pounders designed by Captain Thomas Blomefield. At first fired from the Castle, the noontime signal has boomed out daily in Cape Town from one of these guns since 1806. In the 19th century, such a time signal was particularly important since pocket watches were scarce and often inaccurate. With the advent of the galvanic (or electronic) telegraph, it became possible to trigger the guns remotely, and since 1864, the noon gun has been accurately fired from the master clock of the South African Astronomical Observatory.

With time, as Cape Town developed and grew, the noise from the guns became too much for the city centre and the guns were moved to their current location at Lion Battery on Signal Hill. The first firing from here was on 4 August 1902. The guns are loaded every day by the South African Navy at about 11:30 with a 3.1-kilogram bag of gunpowder. At noon, prepare yourself for a very loud bang!

The Noon Gun, Lion Battery

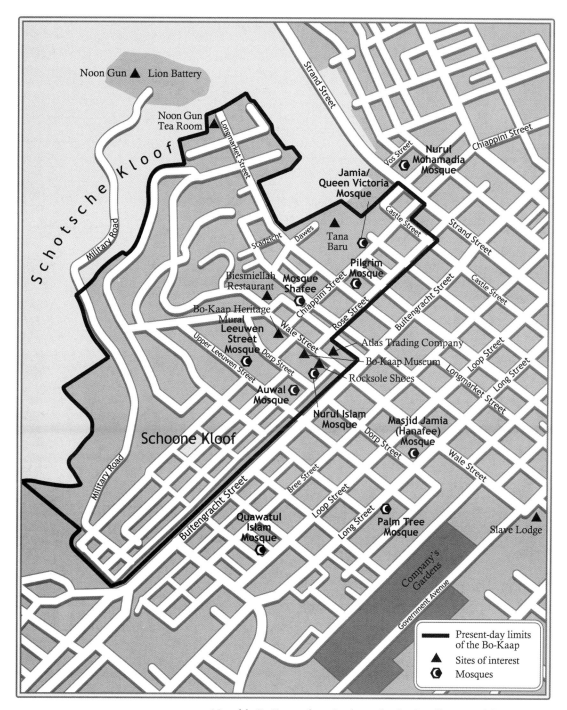

Noon Gun ▲ Lion Battery

Noon Gun
Tea Room

Longmarket Street

Schotsche Kloof

Military Road

Stadzicht

Dawes

Jamia/
Queen Victoria
Mosque

Nurul
Mohamadia
Mosque

Vos Street

Chiappini Street

Castle Street

Strand Street

Tana
Baru

Pilgrim
Mosque

Biesmiellah
Restaurant

Mosque
Shafee

Chiappini Street

Rose Street

Buitengracht Street

Castle Street

Bo-Kaap Heritage
Mural
Leeuwen
Street
Mosque

Upper Leeuwen Street

Dorp Street

Wale Street

Atlas Trading Company

Bo-Kaap Museum

Rocksole Shoes

Longmarket Street

Loop Street

Long Street

Auwal
Mosque

Nurul Islam
Mosque

Dorp Street

Masjid Jamia
(Hanafee)
Mosque

Wale Street

Schoone Kloof

Military Road

Buitengracht Street

Bree Street

Loop Street

Long Street

Quawatul
Islam
Mosque

Palm Tree
Mosque

Slave Lodge

Company's
Gardens

Government Avenue

Strand Street

——— Present-day limits
of the Bo-Kaap

▲ Sites of interest

☾ Mosques

Map of the Bo-Kaap and associated area, showing sites of interest and the ten mosques

The Spice Trade

NUTMEG

GINGER

London
Amsterdam
EUROPE
ASIA
CHINA
Basra
Hormuz
Ts'uan-cho
Berenice
ARABIA
Barygaza
Tongking
AFRICA
Adulis
Muza
INDIA
Muziris
CEYLON
MALAYA
Equator
SUMATRA
ZANZIBAR
Bantam
Rhapta
INDIAN OCEAN
Batavia (Jakarta)
JAVA
ATLANTIC OCEAN
MADAGASCAR
MAURITIUS

Cape Town

Maritime Spice Routes
from Southeast Asia

Spice route to Europe
Cinnamon route
Clove route

Of Slaves and Spices

꒰ꙮ꒱

The heart of a slave in bondage

꒰ꙮ꒱

Dark and dreary in a world of isolation
Torn away from kith and kin
Into bondage captured – strangled in spirit
A life of submission to the masters' whim

Where are our sisters, mothers and fathers?
In this strange land, alone and forlorn
Through greed and lustful desires
Our lives have become so brutally torn

Far in the distant future
We long for a change of heart
Life has a way of rebalancing
Destiny may yet play a kinder part

Abdeya da Costa

Slavery's heritage
A rich cuisine

*C*ape Town is truly blessed. This region was not described as 'the Fairest Cape' without good reason. Table Mountain stands guard over one of the most beautiful cities in the world, where architecture ranges from colonial Cape Dutch and Malay through Georgian and Victorian to ultramodern. A vast array of restaurants serve up international cuisine of the highest calibre, and just beyond the CBD stretch the world-famous Cape winelands.

All this opulence and fine dining comes at a price, though. It's hard to reconcile the fact that if it were not for the Spice Route and the slave trade, there would have been little opportunity to relax in one of our graceful Cape Dutch manor houses, enjoying a spicy meal cooked to perfection whilst relishing in the grandeur of the cultivated vineyards.

In 1498, Vasco da Gama, a well-known figure in the history of the Cape, arrived in Calicut along the Malabar Coast of India and activated a process that led, eventually, to several European countries being given the power of control over commercial activities of countries bordering the eastern Indian Ocean. One of the major power players was the Netherlands. As a result, this region was named the Dutch East Indies, and monitored by the Dutch East India Company, or Verenigde Oostindische Compagnie (VOC).

Spices, freely available in the East Indies, became an extremely tradable commodity. Europeans gained a taste for the exotic and a spice trade rapidly began to develop. However, with the vast distances to be sailed between Europe and the East Indies, it was necessary to have refuelling ports of call. Thus, in 1652, when the VOC set up a halfway station at the Cape, they had no real intention to colonise the region.

Groot Constantia Manor House –
a fine example of Cape Dutch architecture

EXILES IN A FOREIGN LAND

Almost hand in glove with the Spice Route was the slave trade. Colonial valour made conquering new lands and the expansion of the kingdom highly desirable. Along with this land acquisition came the people, who were viewed as yet another type of tradable commodity. Morality didn't enter into the equation – a workforce was required and they were there for the capturing.

The following table gives an indication of the composition of the slave population in Cape Town during the period 1652–1818.

Place of Origin	Percentage Derived from Country
Africa	26.65 %
Ceylon	3.10 %
India	36.40 %
East Indies	31.47 %
Mauritius	0.18 %
Malaya	0.49 %
Others	0.40 %
Unidentified	1.31 %

Source: Pages from Cape Muslim History, *by Yusuf da Costa and Achmat David (Shuter & Shooter)*

The earliest groups of Muslims to come to the Cape formed a constituent of the vast influx of slaves, criminals and political exiles. They came aboard seafaring galleys such as *De Voetboeg*, which arrived at the Cape on 2 April 1694 en route from Ceylon. This vessel's particular consignment included 49 Muslim exiles from the East Indies, one of whom was Sheikh Yusuf of Macassar, who later became a major Muslim religious leader at the Cape. Included in the number were the *mardyckers*, or Malay servants of the VOC officials on their way back to the Netherlands from the Dutch East Indies. But in the end, the Cape became their home.

A vibrant community began to develop in Cape Town. Many of the slaves and exiles were also skilled artisans and builders. The Bo-Kaap, among the oldest areas in Cape Town, reflects the eclectic mix of the immigrant population at that time through its architecture, ranging from Dutch and British influences to classical Eastern styles. Another distinguishing feature of the Bo-Kaap is its many mosques, built by free Muslims and Muslim slaves to serve as places of worship for the community.

*The Auwal Mosque in Dorp Street –
Cape Town's oldest mosque*

Zanzibar
The heart of slavery

Zanzibar. The very word conjures up magical images of adventure and Arabian nights; one might expect it to be a place of fantasy. However, ask any traveller who has been there and they will confirm that it is very much a real place, filled with island wonders. Actually, Zanzibar is an archipelago of islands lying 35 kilometres east of the coast of Tanzania. The correct name for the island referred to as 'Zanzibar' is Unguja, which is close to its sister island Pemba, and a number of smaller islands and coral atolls.

The link between Zanzibar and the Bo-Kaap may not at first be obvious. Zanzibar was the hub for both the Spice Route and the slave trade, and many of the slaves arriving in Cape Town came via Zanzibar. Many more died on the island or perished en route. Stone Town, Zanzibar's capital, is a permanent reminder of just how horrific the trade in human lives was. Twenty kilometres (12 miles) north of it is a large cave. Mangapwani, which means 'Arab shore', has a beautiful stretch of coastline that gives no hint of the slave chamber that lies buried in the rocks. Descending the steep steps leading into the belly of the earth one experiences a palpable feeling of hell – the souls of the dead crying in torment. This chamber was created by Mohamed bin Nassor to hide his slaves well away from the prying British anti-slavery patrols. Many of the slaves who went into the chamber were never to see the light of day again.

Tippu Tip was known in Zanzibar as East Africa's most feared slave trader. His real name was Hamed bin Muhammed al-Murjebi. Born in 1830, he was the son of an Arab plantation owner. His nickname 'Tippu Tip' comes from an East African bird whose eyes constantly blink; many people saw a resemblance in his pronounced facial twitch.

In the late 1860s, at the height of his success – the result of a combination of ruthless ambition, cruelty, greed and financial astuteness – he was leading slave caravans of over 4000 men. The site of the Old Slave Market in Stone Town lies adjacent to the Anglican Cathedral Church of Christ. In the courtyard is a sculpture of five slaves within a pit, bound together by chains – lest we forget.

Zanzibar is also redolent of the spices growing in the higgledy-piggledy plantations (*shamba*). Towering coconut palms mingle with vanilla plants and pineapple, and the unmistakable smell of cloves fills the air as they crackle underfoot.

View of Stone Town

The Mangapwani Slave Chamber and Slave Monument

Crime and Punishment

Illustration of a slave being whipped

In his book *Cape of Torments*, Robert Ross gives the following account of the type of physical control to which slaves were often subjected:

It is true that at the Cape the slave-owners themselves were forbidden to punish their slaves beyond a certain degree. They could only employ what was appropriate for 'domestic correction'. The slaves could even enter complaints with the central government when they considered this norm to have been exceeded. The government of the Dutch East India Company was concerned to maintain the monopoly of force in its own hands. This did not mean that the slaves were able to escape from the rigours of exceedingly vigorous punishment. They could be sent by the owners to the fiscaal *(the public prosecutor and head of the police) or to the local magistrate to be flogged or to work on the treadmill, more or less at their owner's discretion. For more serious offences they were subject to a legal system that exacted punishments of the utmost barbarity. Slaves convicted of theft were likely to be hanged. Those who had murdered other slaves or Khoikhoi would be broken on a wheel, with the 'coup de grace' (from the French, literally 'mercy blow'). Killing a white would elicit the same punishment without the coup de grace, and in particularly violent cases this would be preceded by tearing eight pieces of the unfortunate slave's flesh away with red-hot pincers. When the victim was the slave's own master, even this was not enough. The condemned man would be impaled on a stake driven up his anus and left to die. If he were lucky, he would become unconscious in about two days.*

At the Cape, the lives of the slaves were subject to strict control. To prevent them from rising up against their masters, a Slave Code was drawn up, to which slaves had to adhere.

The Cape Slave Code of 1754

Slaves are to be indoors after 10pm or carry a lantern at night. Thus slaves are not permitted to be on the street at night after 10pm without a torch. [Added in 1760]

Slaves are not to ride horses nor wagons in the streets.

Slaves are not to sing, whistle or make any other sound at night. Thus slaves are not allowed to whistle loudly, and thereby entice other slaves from their masters' homes.

Slaves are not to meet in bars, buy alcohol, or form groups on public holidays.

Slaves are not to gather near entrances of a church during the time of religious services being conducted.

Slaves are not to stop in the street to talk to other slaves.

Slaves who insult or falsely accuse a freeman will be flogged. Thus slaves are not permitted to be cheeky with any slave-owner in public.

Slaves who strike a slaveholder will be put to death.

Slaves are not permitted to own guns or to carry dangerous weapons. [Added in 1686]

Free Blacks are not equal to White Free Burghers.

Freed slave women are not to wear coloured silk or hoop skirts, fine lace, or any decoration on their hats, or earrings made of gems or imitation gems. [Added in 1765]

Slaves are banned from public assemblies in groups of 3, 4 or more in the streets or anywhere else. Law enforcement officials have standing instructions to disperse any crowd of slaves of 3 or more. [Added in 1696]

No slave nor anyone else is permitted to walk about with a burning tobacco pipe in public – in order to prevent fires.

Source: The Slave Book by R Jacobs (Kwela Publishers)

The CSS Alabama

The CSS *Alabama* holds a special place in the history of the Cape. A ship of war built in 1862, during the American Civil War for the Confederacy by John Laird Sons & Company, Liverpool, UK, it was launched initially as *Enrica*, fitted out as a cruiser, and then commissioned on 24 August 1862 as CSS *Alabama*. A mixed crew of British mercenaries and Southern white sailors was assembled to man the ship. Also on board was a small contingent of African-American slaves who served as cleaners and mess stewards; they also provided musical entertainment for the crew.

Once commissioned, the *Alabama*, under Captain Raphael Semmes, spent the next two months capturing and burning ships in the North Atlantic and intercepting American grain ships bound for Europe. This trail of destruction continued through the West Indies, where the *Alabama* sank USS *Hatteras* along the Texas coast and captured her crew. The *Alabama* also patrolled the South Atlantic, where it would wait for Union ships to come around the Cape from the Far East, on their way to the east coast ports of Philadelphia, New York, Newport and Boston. It would then attack, plunder and sink them. The *Alabama* was one of the most notorious and feared Southern commerce raiders on patrol in the South Atlantic, sending a total of 58 Union ships to the bottom of the ocean during her two-year patrol.

On a subsequent voyage, the *Alabama* docked in Cape Town to replenish supplies, and the local population flocked to the harbour to have a look at this grand ship. It was the first time the inhabitants of Cape Town had had informal contact with African-Americans. Dressed in their minstrel outfits, the slaves gave impromptu musical recitals on the dockside where the *Alabama* was moored. Upon seeing this spectacle, some of the locals enquired from the white crew who these black entertainers were. The reply: 'These are simply our Coons!'

Despite the term being a derogatory one in the vernacular, similar to that of 'nigger', the word stuck. So did the form of entertainment, leading eventually to the Coon Carnival, a popular festival in Cape Town at the start of January every year.

On 11 June 1864, the *Alabama* arrived in Cherbourg, France, and Captain Semmes requested permission to dock to overhaul his ship. In pursuit of the raider, the American ship of war USS

Kearsarge arrived three days later and took up a patrol just outside the harbour. On 19 June, the *Alabama* sailed out to meet the *Kearsarge*, and as the latter turned to meet its opponent, the *Alabama* opened fire. The *Kearsarge* waited patiently until the range had closed to less than 1000 yards. According to the survivors, the two ships steamed on opposite courses, moving around in circles as each commander tried to cross the bow of his opponent to deliver a heavy raking fire. Suddenly a shell fired by the *Kearsarge* tore open a section at the *Alabama*'s waterline. The water rushed through the cruiser, forcing it to the ocean floor. While the *Kearsarge* rescued most of the *Alabama*'s survivors, Captain Semmes and 41 others were picked up by the British yacht *Deerhound* and escaped to England.

Painting by Durand-Brager – Battle of the USS Kearsage *and the CSS* Alabama *1864*

SLAVERY BECOMES PERMANENT AT THE CAPE

From the time the first slaves arrived at the Cape on 28 March 1658, the VOC was faced with a major problem. Where were they going to put them? The only conceivable solution at the time was to accommodate their human cargo at the fort. The Fort de Goede Hoop had been built just after Jan van Riebeeck's arrival at the Cape, and was later replaced by the present-day Castle. This arrangement proved far from satisfactory, so a purpose-built Slave Lodge was erected near to the Company Gardens. All the rooms of the building opened onto a central courtyard, where a daily roll call and any announcements took place. The Slave Lodge thus acted as a 'storage' facility from where slaves were on-sold. This practice remained in operation for nearly 131 years, until 1808 when the British outlawed the oceanic slave trade.

The Old Slave Lodge

Timeline of the African Slave Trade			
1451–1600	**Beginning of the African slave trade**	1791	Slave trade opened to free enterprise
1451	Africans captured in West Africa taken to Europe by the Portuguese	1795	British take over the Cape Colony and torture is abolished
1518	Spanish bring slaves to the Caribbean	1802	Slavery and the slave trade reinstituted in the French Empire by Napoleon
1600–1700	**Slave trade grows**	1808	Oceanic slave trade outlawed by British
1619	20 Africans sold to settlers in British colony of Virginia	**1811–1870**	**Slave trade declines**
1652	VOC establishes a refreshment station at the Cape	1820	Last state in the northern United States declares slavery illegal
1658	First major batch of slaves arrives at the Cape	1834	Abolition of slavery in British colonies, beginning of slave apprenticeship
1700–1811	**Slave trade peaks**	1838	Period of mandatory 'apprenticeship' for adult ex-slaves ends
1700	Government directive restricts male slaves being brought from the East	1848	Second emancipation of slaves in the French Empire
1772	Slavery outlawed for individuals in Britain	1862	Emancipation Proclamation in the United States; all slaves in the Southern states are set free
1787	First emancipation of slaves in the French Empire		

Source: Dates taken from the Educator's Guide to the UNESCO General History of Africa and Slavery in the Cape Colony *by Alistair Boddy-Evans*

Spices
The flavour of the Bo-Kaap

The ancient Greek word for 'spice' was the precursor of our word 'aroma'. Nicely packaged and relatively inexpensive, these fragrant bits of bark, leaves and seeds were once so costly that men were willing to risk their lives in order to bring back their precious cargo. Archaeologists estimate that by 50 000BCE primitive humans had discovered that parts of certain aromatic plants could help to make food taste better, and so began a trade that has flourished to this day.

From the hieroglyphics on the walls of the pyramids, to the scriptures of the Qur'an and the Bible, there is frequent mention of the important role of spices. The great trade routes of antiquity carried caravans with as many as 4000 camels bearing spices and the rich merchandise of the East, plodding along from Goa, Calicut and the Orient to spice markets in Nineveh, Babylon, Carthage, Alexandria and Rome. Arabs were the masters of this dangerous yet highly lucrative trade. Along with the advent of Islam came a greater impetus for spice trading. The prophet Mohammad married a wealthy spice-trading widow and, as his missionaries made their way throughout Asia spreading their faith, they also collected spices.

Whether spices came by sea or by land, they had to pass through Cairo, and from there they were shipped to Alexandria. At this major port spices were bought and shipped by the Venetians and the Genoese. In 1271, Marco Polo, a young Venetian, set out with his father and uncle on a 24-year journey that was to take them all over Asia, as far as fabled Cathay, or China. Marco Polo's voyage lead to the European discovery of the New World and opened up trade with the Orient. Suddenly European merchants realised that these places could be reached by ship and the race was on. First Portugal, followed by Spain and England, then Holland vied for control of the Spice Route, with the subsequent establishment of English and Dutch East India Companies.

By 1600 the British East India Company had been chartered by Queen Elizabeth, with spice cargoes as the main objective. Whilst the Dutch controlled the East Indies, the English were gaining supremacy on the mainland of India itself. Then in 1780, the Dutch and the English fought a war that was to herald the beginning of the end for the Dutch East India Company. In 1795 the English took control of Malacca and a year later all Dutch property and trading centres except for Java. The Dutch East India Company was finally dissolved in 1799.

During his time at the Cape, the Dutch governor Jan van Riebeeck set up the Company Gardens to provide fruit and vegetables for both passing ships and the fledgling settlement at the foot of the mountain. However, it was the slaves who had been captured in the East Indies, India and Ceylon who brought from their native lands their traditional recipes and were responsible for the spicy curries, *sosaties* and hot *atjars* that have become synonymous with the cuisine and flavour of the Bo-Kaap today.

LEGACY OF THE SPICE ROUTE

Most kitchen cupboards feature spices in some shape or form – but do you ever stop to think about how they're blended or processed or where they come from? The truth is, the reason we have such a tantalising selection of spices available to us today is due to the considerable influence of the Spice Route and accompanying slave trade. The secrets of some of Atlas Trading Company's most popular spices are divulged below.

Allspice/Jamaican pepper, or Pimento *(Pimento dioica)*

It has been given this name because it tastes like a combination of ground pepper, cinnamon, nutmeg and cloves. It's derived from the berries of the pimento tree, which reaches a height of about 8 metres and grows on the Caribbean islands.

Cloves *(Eugenia caryophyllata)*

The word 'clove' is derived from the Latin word *clavis*, which means 'nail'. They are the closed flower buds of a cone-shaped tree, which grows to a height of around 7 metres. Clove trees are plentiful in Zanzibar, and also occur in the Philippines, Mauritius and Madagascar.

Cardamom *(Elettaria cardamomum)*

This is the second most valuable spice next to saffron; it may be sold as whole seeds or in ground form. The cardamom plant is a member of the ginger family, and grows best in warm, tropical climates in countries and islands of the Indian Ocean. Its taste is similar to eucalyptus and is used in many curry dishes and for adding flavour to meat and soup.

Cinnamon *(Cinnamomum zeylanicum)*

The spice actually consists of the bark from trees of the laurel family, originating in Sri Lanka. The tree can grow to gigantic proportions – up to 90 metres. The bark, when removed, is rolled into short sticks or ground to a powder. It's a very popular spice, not just amongst the Malay community but also worldwide, and it's sure to be found in most kitchens.

Cumin/Jeera *(Cuminum cyminum)*

It may be a surprise to discover that this is a member of the carrot family! The flavour of cumin is very similar to that of caraway seeds; it's a popular component of curries.

Turmeric/Borrie *(Curcuma longa)*

A member of the ginger family, this tuberous root is bright yellow on the outside, orange-brown on the inside; it has a similar taste to mustard. India produces the greatest quantities of turmeric. It's used for medical as well as flavouring and colouring purposes.

Garlic *(Allium sativum)*
Common to every cook, garlic was originally known only for its medicinal properties. Love it or hate it, pungent garlic adds a unique flavour to most dishes.

Chilli *(Capsicum frutescens longum)*
Although common throughout the world today, chillies originally came from South America and India. They are available in a range of strengths, from very mild to extra hot and spicy. When chilli is dried and powdered, it's called red or cayenne pepper. It's the main ingredient of curry powder.

Bay leaves *(Laurus nobilis)*
The laurel tree has a typical pyramid shape and originally came from countries bordering onto the Mediterranean Sea. Leaves may be used in many dishes, fresh or dry.

Coriander/Dhania/Kolyanna
(Coriandrum sativum)
Coriander seeds and leaves are used in a variety of dishes. Indigenous to North Africa and Asia, the plant grows about 1 metre tall, bearing bright green seeds that ripen to a red-violet colour. The fragrant smell is similar to sage and lemon.

Saffron *(Crocus sativus)*
This member of the crocus family is the rarest and most expensive of the spices. The name comes from the Arabian word *za'faran*, meaning 'yellow', describing the bright colour of the stamens. Some idea of why this spice is so expensive is gleaned when you understand that it takes 7500 flowers to produce just 4.5 grams of dried saffron.

Fenugreek/Methi/Meti *(Trigonella foenum graecum)*
The ancient Egyptians used this plant as an aphrodisiac. Cultivated in India and Asia, it thrives in a warm climate and damp soil. It often forms part of the curry powder mix and is an ingredient in vanilla essence.

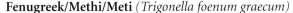

Atlas Trading Company
A personal story

Situated at 94 Wale Street, Atlas Trading Company are wholesale merchants who are the main suppliers of exotic spices for Cape Town's southern suburbs. Their customers are divided between domestic households, restaurants and hotels. The story of the company reflects the interesting nature of the spice trade, the blend of cultures in the Bo-Kaap and changing forces throughout the years, from apartheid to the present.

In 1895, Mr Ahmed, grandfather of Atlas Trading Company's current owners, arrived from Bombay to seek a new life in the Cape. Whereas many Indian families who settled in Durban were brought as forced labour to work on the sugar plantations, those who arrived in Cape Town became artisans and shopkeepers. Mr Ahmed opened a corner shop in the Bo-Kaap, which was in turn run by his sons. In the early part of the 20th century, there were

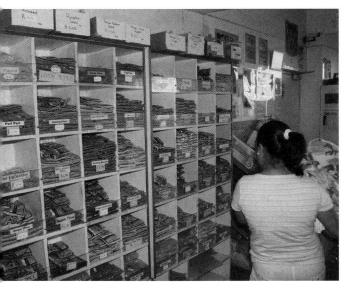

many more Indian corner shops in the Bo- Kaap. The decline today of this type of trading is possibly a reflection of greater educational opportunities available, and also the pressure of larger businesses and the omnipresent shopping centres.

Originally, a Mr Basson owned the business that became known as Atlas Trading Company. At that time it was a wholesale grocery outlet; very few spices were traded and those that were, were all imported from India. In 1946, Mr Ahmed's sons, the father and uncle of the current proprietors, bought the business. A growing local market for spices reflected the increasing diversity of cuisine in the Cape, and spices were now imported from Thailand, Bangkok and the Middle East, as well as from India.

Then, following the establishment of the apartheid government, there were international sanctions. It was no longer possible to get spices directly from India and Indonesia, so a plan was implemented to transfer the Indian spices to another container in Singapore. Only after the end of apartheid were relationships once more re-established with both India and Indonesia.

The Group Areas Act introduced during 1950 also put pressure on traders. Up until this time the Bo-Kaap, like District Six, had existed as a happy microcosm of multiculturalism. Then District Six was declared a 'White Area', and many forced evictions took place; the Bo-Kaap was designated a 'Malay Area'. This meant that people from ethnic groups other than Malay were required to live elsewhere, and they required a government-issued permit to continue their business in the Bo-Kaap. During this period many Indian families moved to Rylands Estate, which had been designated an 'Indian Area'.

The current owners entered into the business in 1971. It has since diversified and now also acts as an outlet for Islamic literature. Wahab Ahmed, one of the directors of Atlas Trading, while pondering on life in the Bo-Kaap, says, 'The cultural diversity and religious tolerance in the area are again back to what was here before the years of apartheid. We are a Muslim family, but we happily coexist with our Hindu and Christian neighbours. There is a lot of religious tolerance within the Bo-Kaap and a desire to live together in harmony and share our cultures. Much like a blend of spices, each one is unique, but in its own way, vital in giving flavour to the dish.'

Keeping an Aromatic Kitchen

ɞଵେ

On Eating and Drinking

ɞଵେ

Then an old man, a keeper of an inn, said,
Speak to us of Eating and Drinking.
And he said:
Would that you could live on the fragrance
of the earth, and like an air plant be sustained
by the light.
But since you must kill to eat, and rob
the newly born of its mother's milk to quench
your thirst, let it then be an act of worship,
And let your board stand as an altar on which
the pure and the innocent of forest and plain
are sacrificed for that which is purer and
still more innocent in man.

Source: The Prophet *by Kahlil Gibran*

Food
The key to celebrations and feasts

Within Muslim communities the world over, the preparation of food dishes is intimately connected to rites of passage and religious festivals. For non-Muslim readers, the descriptions that follow serve as a very basic summary of some of the most significant celebrations.

Ramadan

The festival of *Ramadan* falls in the ninth month of the Muslim calendar and lasts for that entire month. It is the most important religious fast, when the faithful abstain from all food and drink between sunrise and the sighting of the moon each evening. (See also Fast of *Ramadan*, page 62) Children may begin to observe this fast as early as seven years of age, but will definitely be accustomed to fasting by the year of their 15th birthday.

After sundown, dates or *vetkoek* (a dough deep-fried in oil) are eaten before the men go to the mosque. On their return the family joins in a meal usually composed of *bredie* (stew) or soup. During the fast, on Thursday and Sunday evenings, *boeber* (milky drink) is served.

The 27th night of *Ramadan* – or 'Night of Power' – is considered the holiest night. It is also referred to as '*Kersopsteek*', which means 'to light candles', so it may also be spoken of as 'Night of Light'. A special meal is prepared, which may include many of the dishes featured in the recipe section (pages 40–52). To the faithful, this is the night when their sins are forgiven.

Eid-ul-fitr (Feast of *Labarang*)

This feast begins on the last day of *Ramadan*, with the first sighting of the moon by the *imam*. Very occasionally if, on this evening, there is no clear view of the moon, the *imam* will delay *Eid* until the moon is obvious. Once the moon is clearly sighted, the men will wash and dress, then go to the mosque to hear the *imam* reciting from the Qur'an. Compulsory alms, called *fitra*, are taken to the mosque to be given to the priests and the poor, to commemorate *Eid*, or the feast of *Labarang*.

At this time many dishes with rice are prepared, including *biryani*, curries, butter chicken or *tandoori* chicken, *bredie* and spicy rice.

Tamat

This is a big day in every young Muslim's life. As part of their religious education they are taught by the *imam* to speak Arabic and recite from the Qur'an. At the end of their training period they are given an oral examination by the *imam* on aspects of the Qur'an, in front of an audience. This represents their entry into adulthood and culminates with a feast at the mosque. *Biryani* and spicy rice are very popular on this special occasion.

Preparing for the tamat – *Boys'* madrassah *class in 1938*

Korbaan

Korbaan, 'the Day of Sacrifice', takes place about 70 days after the end of *Ramadan*. Families who can afford it arrange to sacrifice a goat to commemorate Abraham being called by the Divine to sacrifice his son Isaac, at which time a sacrificial lamb was provided in Abraham's son's place. In modern-day ceremonies, the requirements are that the animal is less than a year old, without blemish, and is also not pregnant.

Once slaughtered, the carcass is cut up and the meat distributed to the needy. The person providing the animal only receives the pluck (heart, liver and lungs). Family, friends and neighbours may offer contributions of food for the celebration meal that follows the sacrifice. This meal normally features *biryani* and offal.

Feast of the Orange Leaves

This festival is known as 'cutting *rampi*' – or in the Afrikaans language, *rampi-sny* (*rampi* being a Malay term for 'mixture'). What gets cut up are the leaves of an orange tree as the Prophet Muhammad was said to have been covered in orange leaves at his birth.

On this occasion, women are permitted into the main part of the mosque, where they sit on the floor with knives and chopping boards. Orange leaves (banana or fig leaves may also be used) are cut up and placed in communal piles in large dishes on the floor. The wife of the *imam* pours expensive oil onto the leaves and works it through with her hands. The pile of leaves is then covered with a cloth and the entire bundle steamed, allowing the exotic aromatic fragrance to permeate the mosque.

Once steamed the leaves are divided into small portions and put into sachets. In the evening when the men come to the mosque to pray, each is given one of these sachets to place in his breast pocket. After prayers, the feasting begins with curry dishes and spicy rice flanked with special flavoursome Malay condiments.

Goats wandering through the Bo-Kaap prior to Korbaan

Doepmaal (The Name-giving Feast)

The name-giving ceremony affords yet another opportunity to prepare a sumptuous feast to share with family and friends. *Doepmaal* is usually held in the parents' home seven days after the birth of the child. During the name-giving ceremony the *imam* holds a sweet date to the baby's lips while his or her name is said aloud and prayers are offered. At the family gathering afterwards, *bobotie* and fried vermicelli are popular dishes.

Women preparing for the Feast of the Orange Leaves in the Queen Victoria Mosque

The following recipes, which feature in many celebrations in the Bo-Kaap,
have been kindly provided by Atlas Trading Company. Most serve approximately 6–8 people.

SPICY RICE

Meat and rice form the staple diet for many living in the Bo-Kaap. Some may view rice, perhaps, as rather bland, but this Malay recipe proves that with a little flair, rice can be turned into something magical and exotic. Spicy rice beautifully accompanies curries, chicken dishes or *sosaties*.

Ingredients

400g (500ml) rice
4 cloves
4 cardamom seeds
3 small pieces of stick cinnamon
Pinch of ground allspice
Salt to taste
Oil
1 medium-sized onion, cut into thin rings
Cumin seeds
Ground coconut
Flaked almonds
Raisins

Method

~ Put rice in saucepan of boiling water and start cooking, stirring occasionally. Add spices and salt to taste. Cook uncovered for 10–12 minutes. Drain rice in a colander and place in the saucepan again.
~ Heat oil, then brown the onion rings and sprinkle cumin seeds over them. Place onions on top of rice and place in oven at 150°C to dry slightly. To ensure a light fluffy texture, use a fork to 'loosen' the rice and mix the onions through. Sprinkle coconut, flaked almonds and raisins over the top before serving.

BOEBER

Boeber **is a sweet milky drink that came originally from Java, and was made with coconut milk. The consistency can vary from that of gruel to a thickness that needs a spoon. Traditionally it is prepared in the morning and drunk on Thursday and Sunday evenings, but it's also drunk on a cold winter's night. It is always served on the 15th night of *Ramadan*, although it's a favourite drink at most festive occasions. Many Cape Malay recipes exist, and most now substitute cow's milk for coconut milk.**

Ingredients

150g butter
200g vermicelli
2 litres cow's milk
2 cinnamon sticks, bruised
10 cardamom seeds, bruised
Sugar to taste
Rose water or vanilla essence for flavouring
Approx. 70g (100ml) sago
1 tin sweetened condensed milk

Method

~ Melt butter in a saucepan and brown the vermicelli in it. Add the milk, cinnamon sticks and cardamom and bring to the boil, then reduce heat. Add sugar and rose water or vanilla essence to taste.
~ Stir in the sago and simmer until done, increasing the amount of sago to thicken as required. Add condensed milk, stirring continuously to mix, and then serve.

CURRIES

Curry dishes originating in Java tend to be cooked in coconut pulp or coconut oil, whereas those of Bengalese or Indian origin are cooked in clarified butter, termed *ghee*. There is a difference within South Africa, too, between curry dishes of the Natal Indian communities and those from the Malay Quarter. Although a great variety of recipes exist, from meat and fish to vegetarian, the following selection of Bo-Kaap curries hopefully caters to all tastes.

Leaf Masala Curry

Ingredients

200g onions
200g tomatoes
1t finely crushed fresh garlic
1t finely crushed fresh ginger (alternatively 2t garlic and ginger paste)
1kg meat or chicken, diced
2T Leaf Masala Mix*
2–3 cups warm water

Method

~ Braise onions until golden brown. Braise tomatoes and add to the onions. Add 1t fine garlic and 1t fine ginger (alternatively 2t garlic and ginger paste). Add diced meat or chicken and cook until nearly done. Stir well in pot and add 2T Leaf Masala Mix. Add 2–3 cups warm water, bring quickly to the boil, then reduce heat to simmer for a few minutes until the sauce has thickened.

* *Available from Atlas Trading Company. Leaf Masala Mix comprises the following spices: coriander, turmeric, chilli powder, fennel (*bariship*), cumin (*jeera*), cloves, cinnamon, curry leaves, star aniseed, cardamom, allspice, bay leaves.*

Fish Curry

In yesteryear, the Malays were the fish vendors of Cape Town. Traders walking with a pole balanced on their shoulders, carrying a bucket or basket of fish hanging off either end, was a typical sight. When a trader blew on his 'fish horn', the local housewives would come running to see the catch of the day.

Ingredients

1kg linefish
2T oil
1 onion, thinly sliced
3t fish masala
3 ripe tomatoes
6 garlic cloves
1t coarse salt
Juice of half a lemon
1 cup water
A few curry leaves
Green mango or quince, sliced
Green dhania
2 green chillies

Method

~ Wash fish and drain well. Heat oil in a wide saucepan; add onion and fry until golden. Add fish masala and braise for $\frac{1}{2}$ minute.
~ Liquidise tomatoes and garlic and add to pan. Add salt, lemon juice and approx. 1 cup water. Cook for about 5–10 minutes until gravy is thick. Add fish and cook further for 10–15 minutes. Add mango or quince in last 10 minutes of cooking. Garnish with curry leaves, green dhania and chillies, and serve with rice, *dhal* and *roti*.

Fish curry with rice, dhal *and* roti

VEGETARIAN OPTIONS

There is no reason, of course, why curries should only contain meat or fish. An increased awareness of healthy eating, and many people cutting out red meat, poultry or fish from their diets, have inspired tasty vegetarian options. Here are a couple of vegetarian curry alternatives.

Red Lentil Curry

Ingredients

> 200g red lentils, rinsed
> 1 onion, finely chopped
> 2 cloves garlic, crushed
> 10ml olive oil
> 2ml chilli powder
> 5ml ground cumin (jeera)
> 5ml turmeric (borrie)
> 1 large ripe tomato, chopped
> Salt to taste

Method

~ Boil the lentils in sufficient salted water till soft. Drain and set aside.

~ Sauté the onions and garlic in olive oil till soft. Add the chilli powder, cumin and turmeric and stir-fry for another few minutes. Add the chopped tomato, and reduce heat to simmer for a few minutes. Add the lentils and mix well, sprinkling in salt to taste.

Butter Bean Curry

Ingredients

> 2T oil
> 1t whole mustard seeds
> 1t whole cumin (jeera)
> 2 small onions, chopped
> 1 green chilli, chopped
> 2 cloves garlic, chopped
> 1t ginger and garlic paste
> 1t chilli powder
> ½t turmeric (borrie)
> 2 chopped ripe tomatoes
> Salt to taste
> 2 tins butter beans
> 1–2 cups water
> 1t fine dhuma
> 2t lemon juice to taste

Method

~ Heat oil in pan; add mustard seeds and whole cumin. When seeds start popping, add chopped onions, fresh chopped chillies and garlic. Sauté till pink in colour.

~ Add all spices, chopped tomatoes and salt, and simmer until thickish gravy is formed. Add beans and water, and boil for 5–10 minutes till beans are soft. Garnish with *dhuma* and add lemon juice/salt to taste.

~ Serve alone with hot rice, or to accompany fresh fish or chops.

(Reproduced from the National Archive M1077)

TANDOORI CHICKEN

This is a favourite traditional Indian recipe, guaranteed to make your guests beg for more. While not traditionally a Cape Malay dish, it illustrates how cultures have borrowed and blended elements from each other. There are many Indian families living within the Bo-Kaap, adding to its unique mix. If the Bo-Kaap is the 'melting pot of nations', then their cuisine can truly be described as 'flavours of the world'.

Ingredients

1 whole chicken

2 onions

Tomato and pineapple, chopped, or sprigs of fresh coriander to garnish

Marinade

1 cup yoghurt or buttermilk, alternatively $\frac{1}{2}$ cup vinegar

2T cooking oil

1t salt

2t ginger and garlic, crushed together in pestle and mortar

3t Tandoori spice

1 green chilli, crushed

$\frac{1}{2}$t turmeric powder (borrie)

$\frac{1}{2}$t red food colouring (optional – this gives a distinctive russet colour)

1T dhania (coriander) leaves, chopped

Method

~ Split the chicken into 2 or 4 parts, then wash and pat dry.

~ Combine all the marinade ingredients and pour over chicken pieces. Leave for 3–5 hours or overnight.

~ Place the chicken pieces with the marinade in an ovenproof dish and bake in a preheated oven at 180°C for at least one hour. Place dish under the grill, basting with juices until tender. Do not let it dry out. Garnish with either chopped tomato and pineapple or fresh sprigs of coriander. Serve with salad, spicy rice and hot *roti* or baked bread.

SOSATIES

Sosaties are such a common dish in South Africa; it's easy to forget that they were originally introduced by Cape Malay immigrants from the island of Java. They are tasty, easy to make, and excellent as a meal with rice or the perfect accompaniment to *boerewors* and beef at a braai (barbecue). A basic *sosatie* consists of pieces of marinated meat interspersed with meat containing fat, skewered on bamboo or wooden sticks. They are fried or grilled over coals.

Ingredients

1kg beef or lamb, cubed

4 onions

100g butter

50g tamarind

8g curry powder

5g turmeric (borrie)

2 crushed garlic cloves

3 sweet chillies, chopped and seeds removed

Bay leaves or lemon leaves

Oil

Fruit, fresh or dried (pineapple, apricots, etc)

Method

~ Cube and wash meat. Chop onions and braise them in a saucepan with the butter.

~ Prepare the marinade by dissolving the tamarind in boiling water and add curry powder, turmeric, garlic, chopped chillies and bay or lemon leaves. Place cubed meat in the saucepan with the onions. Pour marinade over and leave to soak overnight.

~ Skewer the lean meat, alternating with fatty meat, and fruit on wooden sticks. Fry in oil or braai over coals until cooked.

Sosaties *with dates and mango* atjar

BREDIE

Cape Muslim dishes often come in the form of a *bredie* – a kind of meat and vegetable stew. They are a food component on occasions like *tamat*, the wedding feast, and the funeral meal. The following is a fairly unique example using *waterblommetjies*, a type of edible water-lily flower (*Aponogeton* species) that used to be considered a poor man's food. The tables have turned, and today it has become a delicacy.

Ingredients

2 bunches waterblommetjies
2 medium onions, chopped
Olive oil
1½kg cubed mutton
10g sugar
Salt and pepper to taste
450g potatoes, sliced
250ml water
1 bunch sorrel, chopped

Method

~ Remove the *waterblommetjie* flowers from the stems, wash flowers and soak overnight in salt water or brine. Boil flowers quickly, then drain. They can be cut into smaller pieces.

~ Sauté onions in olive oil in a deep pan until golden brown. Add cubed mutton to the pan, along with sugar, and salt and pepper to taste, and cook. Before meat is fully cooked, add *waterblommetjies* and sliced potatoes together with approximately 250ml water. Simmer until ingredients are cooked, but do not let potatoes turn mushy. Add chopped sorrel and serve with rice.

BUTTER CHICKEN

This popular chicken recipe is also ideal for the braai. One of my favourites, my mouth starts watering just thinking about it!

Ingredients

½ cup natural yoghurt
1T extra virgin olive oil
2t ginger and garlic paste
2T lemon juice
½t powdered cinnamon (tuj)
½t powdered cardamom (elachi)
½t powdered cloves
1½t freshly pounded red chillies
1t crushed black pepper
1t white pepper
1t salt
2 chickens, each split in half
1 can tomato purée
½ cup butter
½ cup cream
Mint to garnish

Sauce

To the tomato purée, add butter and 1T lemon juice. Any leftover marinade from the preparation of the chicken may also be added. Mix in the cream just before serving.

Method

~ Mix yoghurt, olive oil, ginger and garlic paste, 1T lemon juice and all the spices together. Smear mixture over the chicken and allow to marinate for a few hours.

~ To cook, lightly fry or grill the chicken over hot coals. Place chicken on a platter and pour the sauce over it. Serve hot, garnished with mint.

BIRYANI

Biryani **may be considered the 'royal' rice dish of India. If you want to impress – this is the one! It does take quite some time to prepare, but the result should be worth the effort. Traditional recipes are often handed down from one generation to the next, and it's a special celebration when the family comes together to enjoy this dish fit for a king.**

Ingredients

$\frac{1}{2}t$ saffron

1T hot water

2 medium onions

$\frac{1}{2}$ cup olive oil and $\frac{1}{2}$ cup ghee

50g butter

1 chicken, washed and dejointed

$1\frac{1}{2}t$ ginger and garlic paste

1 cup natural yoghurt

2T puréed tomato

2 cinnamon sticks

$\frac{1}{2}t$ turmeric

1t coriander

$1\frac{1}{2}t$ red chillies

1T lemon juice

4 whole green chillies

2 sprigs mint

1t salt (to taste)

2 cups whole black lentils (masoor)

2 cups rice

4 cardamom seeds (elachi)

1t cumin (jeera)

3 hard-boiled eggs

6 small potatoes

$\frac{1}{2}$ cup cold water

Method

~ Crisp saffron strands over a low heat, then crush and steep in 1T hot water. Fry onions in olive oil/ghee and butter to pale golden, drain and cool (keep some aside to garnish at the end).

~ Place clean dejointed chicken in a large bowl, add saffron and smear with ginger and garlic paste. Add yoghurt, tomato purée, spices, lemon juice, whole green chillies, fried onions, and sprigs of mint and allow to marinate for at least one hour.

~ Meanwhile, boil black lentils in salted water till done, and drain in colander. Boil rice with 2 cardamom seeds and half of cumin, then drain when half-done (slightly underdone). The remainder of the cardamom seeds and cumin should be added to the chicken.

~ Hard-boil eggs and peel. Fry potatoes in butter/oil used for frying onions till light yellow in colour. In a large flat-bottomed pot with a lid, put in butter/oil used for frying potatoes, and sprinkle a handful of rice and lentils over the bottom. Arrange the marinated chicken on top, and spread the lentils over the chicken. On top of this, spread potatoes and half of the rice. Place chopped hard-boiled eggs on top and cover with rest of rice. Use some of the saffron to tint a little of this rice, and decorate with remainder of fried onions. Sprinkle with $\frac{1}{2}$ cup of cold water and place lid on top of pot.

~ Place pot over high heat for several minutes until contents start to sizzle, then reduce heat to simmer for 1 hour until all the moisture has evaporated.

BOBOTIE

This well-known dish is a lovely blend of flavours. The use of ground mutton in place of beef results in a coarser texture. If using mutton, it should be browned with the onions before it is mixed with the rest of the ingredients.

Ingredients

2 thick slices of stale white bread (not mouldy!)
1–1½ cups water
2 large onions, chopped
1T vegetable oil
4T butter
800g beef mince
3 cloves garlic, crushed
1T Masala
5t turmeric (borrie)
2t ground cumin

2t ground coriander
3 cloves
Pinch of allspice
½t ground peppercorns
½ cup sultanas
½ cup flaked almonds
2T Mrs Ball's Chutney*
Salt and pepper
6–8 lemon leaves (or 2 bay leaves)
2 beaten eggs
1 cup milk

*   *A famous South African off-the-shelf product*

Method

~ Soak the bread in the water. Fry onions in oil and butter until just transparent. Except for the bread, lemon leaves, milk and eggs, place all other ingredients and the fried onions in a large bowl and mix.

~ Squeeze water from bread, add bread to the above mixture and bind well. Spread this in a greased ovenproof dish.

~ Roll the lemon or bay leaves into spikes and insert into the mixture. Bake in a preheated oven at 180°C for 30 minutes. Lightly beat eggs with milk and pour over meat. Continue baking until egg has set.

Traditional bobotie *served with rice*

MALAY CONDIMENTS
A PINCH OF PIQUANT

Dried Red Chilli *Blatjang*

Ingredients

> 60ml smooth apricot jam
> 250ml brown vinegar
> 100g crushed dried red chillies
> 2t crushed garlic
> 1t salt

Method

~ Simply mix all ingredients together until the result produces a smooth paste.

Mango *Atjar (Achar)*

Ingredients

> 4 green mangoes
> Brine / salt water
> 2 cloves garlic, chopped
> 1t fenugreek
> 1t turmeric (borrie)
> 2 red chillies, chopped
> 500ml olive oil
> 3t curry powder

Method

~ Wash mangoes, leave skin on, and cut flesh away from pips. Cut mango with its skin into smaller chunks. Steep the chunks in very salty water or brine overnight, then pat dry. Fry chopped garlic, fenugreek, turmeric and chopped chillies in a small amount of olive oil.

~ Mix curry powder with 250ml olive oil to form a paste. Cover mango chunks with curry paste and store in sterilised screw-top glass jars. Heat rest of oil in a saucepan, add fried spices and boil. Pour boiling oil mixture over mangoes in the jars. Leave to cool, then screw lids on tightly.

~ The flavour of the *atjar* improves with time and is best left for several weeks

(Reproduced from the National Archive E9147)

The circumambulation of the Ka'bah inside the Great Mosque in Mecca

Islam Arrives at the Cape

୶ଵଚଚ

Five Pillars of Islam

୶ଵଚଚ

*No. 1 **Shahada** (affirmation)*
The faithful are required to recite the creed:
'There is nothing worthy of worship save Allah,
and Muhammad is the Messenger of God.'

*No. 2 **Salaah** (prayer)*
Prayer is vital to the faith, and it is the duty of worshippers
to pray five times each day.

*No. 3 **Siyam** (fasting)*
A fast should be kept throughout the holy month of
Ramadan, except for those who are sick or have other
conditions that would prevent them from fasting.

*No. 4 **Zakat** (alms-giving)*
The faithful should provide alms and give help to
the poor and needy.

*No. 5 **Hajj** (pilgrimage)*
At least once within his or her lifetime, a Muslim who has
the financial means and the way is safe must make the holy
pilgrimage to Mecca.

The Arabic influence

The vast majority of people now living within the Bo-Kaap are Muslim. They retain the religion of their ancestors, which thrives today, as vouched for by the 10 mosques that are within this small area. For non-Muslim readers, the following is a basic summary of the practices and beliefs of *Islam* – Arabic for 'submission' or 'obedience unto God'.

According to Islamic belief the Prophet Muhammad, who was the last in a long line of God's messengers, including those common to the Jewish and Christian traditions, was born in the city of Mecca in 570CE. When Muhammad was 40, he was sitting alone in the wilderness near Mecca. The Angel Gabriel appeared to him and commanded Muhammad to read, but he replied: 'I am not a reader.' So for the next 10 days, Angel Gabriel taught Muhammad the verses of the Qur'an, which he memorised.

Time for reflection on the Qur'an

Islamic scholars believe that this First Revelation occurred on the night of the 27th day of *Ramadan*. This night is called the *Layla al-Qadr* (or the 'night of power'). According to the Qur'an, this is when God determines the course of the world for the following year. For Muslims, the receiving of the Holy Qur'an is the equivalent to the Christian and Jewish beliefs in Moses receiving the Ten Commandments on Mount Sinai.

Arabia, at that time, was a polytheistic society. It was Muhammad who taught that there was one true God, *Allah* (Arabic for 'God'), and that he was the creator of the world and controlled everything in it. *Muslim*, in Arabic, means 'one who gives himself to God' and Muhammad urged such faithful subjects to live according to the rules of the Holy Qur'an and what are termed the Five Pillars of faith.

Arabic text

The Qur'an is traditionally written and read in Arabic. Unlike English, Arabic text is written from right to left. Therefore, when reading, one starts at what the Western world traditionally considers to be the 'back' of the book, working towards the 'front'.

   The Arabic alphabet as we know it today appears highly distinctive; it does, however, have a close connection with other early alphabets such as Latin, Greek, Phoenician, and Aramaic. Arabic has no capital letters as such, and the script comprises 18 distinct letter shapes. The shapes vary slightly depending on whether they are connected to another letter before or after them. The full alphabet of 28 letters is thus created by placing various combinations of dots above or below some of these shapes. Three long vowels are included in written words, while the three short vowels are normally omitted – though they can be indicated by marks above and below letters.

An Islamic student's handwritten text, 1808

ARABIC TRANSLITERATION

أ	'	ض	d
ب	b	ط	t
ت	t	ظ	z
ث	th	ع	'
ج	j	غ	gh
ح	h	ف	f
خ	kh	ق	q
د	d	ك	k
ذ	dh	ل	l
ر	r	م	m
ز	z	ن	n
س	s	و	w
ش	sh	ه	h
ص	s	ي	y

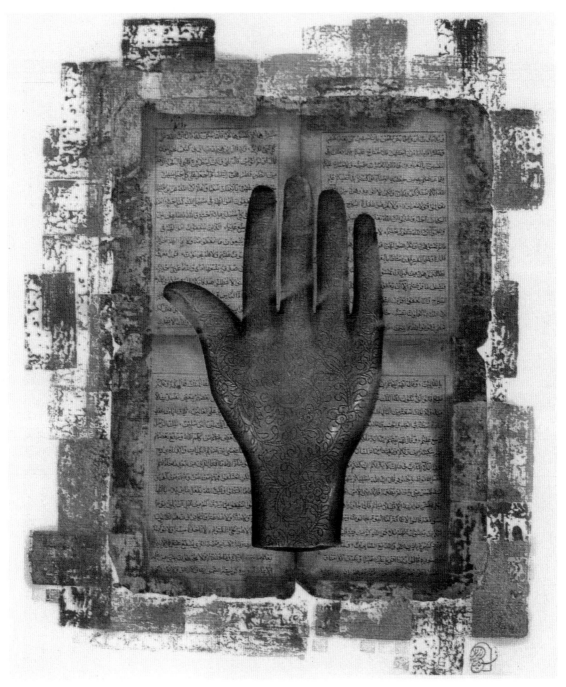

'Blessing to the generous man'
Farideh Zariv, mixed media

HIJRA – THE ISLAMIC CALENDAR

The Islamic calendar began on 16 July 622ᴄᴇ; this is the date on which the Prophet Muhammad emigrated from Mecca to Medina. There are 12 lunar months, alternating between 30 and 29 days, making the year 354 days long – 11 days shorter than the Gregorian calendar. This means that, in general, Islamic fasts and holidays occur 11 days earlier each year.

According to Islam, the 12 months are named *Muharram, Safar, Rabi Owwal, Rabi-ul Akhir, Jumada Owwal, Jumada Agier, Rajab, Shaban, Ramadan, Shawwal, Zulkadah,* and *Dhul Hijjah* (the month of *Hajj*).

The Islamic calendar divides time into cycles that endure for 30 years. During each cycle, 19 years have the regular 354 days; the remaining 11 years each have an extra day. It's interesting to note that the sun, moon and earth all align in the same relative position once every 19 years.

The Islamic measure for a day is the same as that used by the Hebrew culture: it begins at sunset and ends the following sunset. Thus, according to the Qur'an, night is always mentioned before the day.

In order to calculate the beginning of a new lunar month, we need to know the exact time of the 'birth' of the new moon – so we also need to know the exact time of sunset on that day. Theoretically, each new lunar month begins at the birth of the new moon, but in Muslim practice it starts the following sunset. Jewish rabbis used to determine the lunar calendar in much the same way for hundreds of years before the birth of Islam. For nomadic and desert-dwelling people, this also remains a primary means of monitoring the passage of time.

SALAT – DECIPHERING THE ISLAMIC PRAYERS

To the uninitiated, Muslim prayers may appear prolonged and complicated. The following will help to simplify the Islamic act of worship.

Before entering the mosque, shoes are removed and both men and women generally cover their heads. *Fard salat* are the five compulsory prayers, *sunnah* encompass voluntary worship added by the Prophet to the minimum of five daily prayers. Muslims praying together for the *fard* stand as close as possible, shoulders, arms or hips touching. The person who best knows the prayer serves as *imam*, leading the others through the actions of the prayer. The prayers are performed in the Arabic language. *Sunnah* prayers are always made individually.

The five daily prayers occur in repetitions or cycles called *rak'ah*. To begin the *rak'ah*, worshippers stand in the mosque facing the *ka'bah* (a representation of the *Ka'bah* at the centre of the Great Mosque in Mecca), and recite the *sura Fatiha*, which is the first chapter of the Qur'an. It is a prayer of respect to God similar to the 'Lord's Prayer' of the Christian faith and begins, '*Bismillah ar-rahmaan ar-raheem*' ('In the name of God, the Beneficent, the Merciful'). The *sura Fatiha* is followed by additional verses from the Qur'an, recited whilst bowing with hands on the knees, as a sign of worship to the Creator. The person then stands briefly, prostrates him- or herself as an act of submission to God, rises to a kneeling position, prostrates him- or herself again, and finally rises to complete the cycle.

THE FIVE DAILY PRAYERS

Salat al-Fajr (Arabic for 'dawn'), or *subh* (Melayu variation)

This prayer is made at dawn, before sunrise. Two *sunnah* and two *fard* are said, followed by a *salaam*, or 'peace be upon you', said to the person on the right and on the left. Often, portions of the Qur'an are recited after the *fajr* prayer.

Salat al-Thuhr (Arabic for 'noon', when the sun is at its highest)

The second time for prayer, *dhuhr*, happens in the early afternoon, with two *sunnah*, four *fard* and two *sunnah* to end.

Salat al-'Asr (Arabic for 'mid-afternoon')

This is done in the mid-afternoon. *Asr* is like *dhuhr*, but the *sunnah* prayers beforehand are optional, and there are no *sunnah* prayers at the end.

Salat al-'Maghrib (Arabic for 'sunset')

This prayer is made right after sunset. *Maghrib* comprises three *fard* and two *sunnah*. After the first sitting, worshippers stand for a third, silent *rak'ah* (cycle), then sit again and close with *salaams*.

'Isha (Arabic for 'night')

The night prayer, *isha* is made after the red of sunset has left and the sky is dark. *Sunnah* prayers before *isha* are optional, and then four *fard* are said, followed by a group of three *sunnah*, which are referred to as *witr*.

Boys learning to read the Qur'an in tamat *class*

Women gathered at the Queen Victoria Mosque

Sheikh Yusuf (1626–99)

One of the earliest and most prominent Muslim religious leaders in the Cape, Sheikh Yusuf was born in 1626 at Macassar on the island of Celebes (present-day Sulawesi, Indonesia), not far from Goa, India. He lived with his parents until age 18, when he departed on a pilgrimage to Mecca. The holy city proved to be a place of enlightenment for him. Here he learned Arabic and Islamic religious sciences such as *Tafsir al-Qur'an*, *Ahadith* and *Fiqh*. During this time he also memorised the Qur'an, which made him a highly respected scholar of Islam. Whilst in Mecca, Yusuf took two wives before setting sail for Bantam in western Java, where he became a spiritual guide to Sultan Ageng.

By the middle of the 17th century, the Dutch East India Company had managed to establish an almost complete monopoly over politics and trade in the East Indies. There were, however, areas of major resistance against the Dutch – these included the sultanates of Mataram (covering most of Java), Atjeh in Sumatra, and Ternate. Sultan Ageng succeeded in holding out against the colonists, and local trade flourished in Bantam. In 1659, however, the Dutch East India Company blockaded the Bantam trade route, forcing the sultan into a peace agreement – which led to great discord and infighting among the regional sultanates.

As the conflict increased, Sheikh Yusuf remained staunchly loyal to his sultan. But Ageng was ousted from power in 1680 by his own son, Abd al-Qahar (who became known as Sultan Haji). He tried to lead a rebellion against his son and the Dutch, but was forced to surrender in 1683. He went into exile in Batavia (present-day Jakarta, Indonesia) where he died in 1692. Sheikh Yusuf continued to fight the combined force of the Sultan Haji and the Dutch, taking about 4000 followers with him into the mountains of Bantam. Ultimately, however, Sheikh Yusuf was captured and sent to Batavia.

Batavia's loss is the Cape's gain

The Dutch East India Company eventually decided to send him to South Africa, where he arrived in Cape Town on 2 April 1694, with his retinue of 12 *imams*, two wives and his children. In 1994 a major exhibition was staged in Cape Town to mark this event and the effective tricentenary of the arrival of Islam in the Cape. The Dutch, hoping that exile on the remote Cape farm Zandvliet would bring an end to the troublesome Sheikh, underestimated Yusuf's influence. Paramount as spiritual leader of the *Khalwatiyyah* order in the Cape, founded by Umar al-Khalwati, he became a major influence in establishing and spreading the teachings of Islam. Umar al-Khalwati lived in Iran in the 13th century; the name of the order denotes the performance of certain mystical practices in secret.

Sheikh Yusuf is noted for his literary works, written in three languages – Malaysian, Bughanese and Arabic. The works include *Zubdah al-Asrar*, or 'The Essence of Secrets'.

His impact on Cape society, and specifically in the Bo-Kaap, affected three main areas. His inspirational and steadfast character gave encouragement to the multitude of slaves who had been displaced from their places of origin, and inspired a renewed dignity. He also laid the groundwork for the establishment of socio-religious structures amongst the Muslim community. Lastly, through his zealous desire to seek converts to Islam, he increased the numbers of the faith and gave the community strength in numbers and stability.

Sheikh Yusuf died on 23 May 1699. He is remembered as a founding father of the Cape's Muslim community.

THE FAST OF *RAMADAN*

Since each new lunar month is considered to start at sunset, this is the reason for the sighting of the moon being so important to the commencement and ending of the fast of *Ramadan*.

> *'You may eat and drink until the white thread of light becomes distinguishable from the dark thread of night at dawn. Then, you shall fast until sunset.'* [Qur'an 2:187]

Ramadan is the ninth month, according to the Islamic calendar, and this is when, it's believed, the Holy Qur'an *'was sent down from heaven, a guidance unto men, a declaration of direction, and a means of Salvation'*. In accordance with the Muslim faith, this entire month is a time for fasting and contemplation, culminating on the 27th referred to as the, 'night of power', which is described in the Qur'an as *'better than 1000 months'*.

During the *Ramadan* fast, the strict constraints of not eating during daylight hours are imposed on the daily lives of all Muslims. The fast is broken at the end of the day with prayer and a meal called the *iftar*. Following the *iftar*, it is customary for Muslims to go out to visit family and friends.

It is also common, during *Ramadan*, for Muslims to go to the mosque (*masjid*) to spend several hours praying and studying the Qur'an. In addition to the five daily prayers, they recite a special one called the *taraweeh* ('night') prayer. It is usually two to three times as long as the daily prayers, and some Muslims may spend the entire night praying.

RITUALS OF THE *HAJJ*

Hajj literally means to 'travel' – towards God, that is. It also implies an effort to dominate something, in this connection, the self. Conventionally, the term is translated as 'pilgrimage'. Cape Town – second only to Java – has the highest number of pilgrims in proportion to its Muslim population who visit Mecca annually. It's explicitly stated in the Qur'an that every Muslim who is physically and financially able should make the *hajj* to the holy city of Mecca once in his or her lifetime. This is considered to be the culmination of every Muslim's aspirations and religious duties. The pilgrimage occurs every year between the eighth and 13th days of the last month of the Islamic calendar – *Dhul Hijjah*.

The following summary of the *hajj* is adapted from the *The Oxford History of Islam*.

1. Circumambulation of the *Ka'bah*
The *Ka'bah* is a cube-shaped building at the centre of the Great Mosque in Mecca; built into it is the Black Stone, a meteorite believed to have been sent to earth to Abraham by the Angel Gabriel. Pilgrims walk seven times round the *Ka'bah* in an anticlockwise direction; many attempt to touch the Black Stone. They also run seven times along a passageway in the Great Mosque to commemorate the search for water by Hagar, wife of the Prophet Abraham, the Arabic equivalent of whom is Ibrahim.

2. Standing at Arafat
On the ninth day of the month *Dhul Hijjah*, pilgrims go to Arafat, a plain approximately 14.5 kilometres southeast of Mecca. They may listen to a sermon delivered from Mount Arafat, where the Prophet Muhammad gave his own final sermon.

3. Night at Muzdalifah

Pilgrims spend a night in the open at Muzdalifah, near Mecca.

4. Throwing stones ('stoning the Devil')

Pilgrims throw pebbles – usually about 70 – at three spots where Satan is believed to have tempted the Prophet Ismail. This is symbolic to each pilgrim of casting out 'evil'.

5. Sacrifice at Minah

Pilgrims sacrifice an animal (usually a sheep or goat) in commemoration of the incident narrated in the Old Testament where the Prophet Abraham is about to sacrifice his son and God instead accepts a sheep.

Hajj pilgrims walking through Mecca, 1963

6. Repeat circumambulation of the *Ka'bah*.

7. Drinking Zamzam water

Pilgrims drink water from the Zamzam well, inside the Great Mosque. Muslims believe this is where God provided water to Hagar and her son, Ismail, when they were wandering in the desert.

8. Prayers at the Station of Abraham

Pilgrims pray at the Station of Abraham (*Maqam Ibrahim*), where Abraham and Ismail are believed to have prayed after building the *Ka'bah*.

Pilgrims at Muzdalifah, 1963

A Cape in the embrace of Islam

Over 250 years ago, a prophecy claimed that a 'circle of Islam' would exist around the Cape. Many Muslims believe that this circle is formed by the shrines to saints and *Auliyah*, or 'friends of Allah' – all of whom were brought to the Cape as slaves by the Dutch East India Company. These shrines are termed *mazaar*, or more commonly, *kramat*, which has several translations, including 'saint', 'wonder' or 'miracle'. Over 20 exist within the Western Cape; some of the most important are discussed below.

Signal Hill

The 'circle of Islam' referred to in the prophecy begins at the Tana Baru, just above the quarry in Strand Street. (These *kramats* are described in detail on pages 13–15.) Moving up to the ridge of Signal Hill, you will find the grave of Sheikh Mohamed Hassen Ghaibie Shah al Qadri. Where the Kloof Nek Road junction turns off left towards the Table Mountain Cable Station, take the turn-off to the right for Signal Hill Road. About 1 kilometre along this road, a short path off to the left leads up to the shrine, a small green-and-white building encircled by an ornate fence.

The kramat *of Sheikh Mohamed, on Signal Hill*

This is perhaps one of the most well known of the Cape's *kramats* and the faithful are regularly at prayer here. Sheikh Mohamed was a follower of Sheikh Yusuf of Macassar (see page 61).

Near to the *kramat* are the graves of Tuan Nur Ghiri Bawa (also known as Tuan Galieb), Tuan Sayed Sulaiman and Tuan Sayed Osman. They are marked by raised rectangular structures and adorned with brightly coloured satin.

Continuing further along Signal Hill Road to the Boy Scout Camp entrance, the grave of Tuan Kaape-ti-low is situated some distance from the road. Far less ornate than the *kramat* of Sheikh Mohamed, it comprises a small walled-off enclave with the Muslim moon and star emblem built into one wall, the grave sitting in the centre. Tuan Kaape-ti-low, also known as Jawhi Tuan, was from Java, and was a general in Sheikh Yusuf's army.

Oudekraal and Bakoven

Next, along Victoria Road/M6, near to the Twelve Apostles Hotel and Spa at Oudekraal, the grave of Sheikh Noorul Mubeen lies at the top of 99 steps leading up from the main road. A bright green building standing beside a stream greets the breathless climber. If he or she looks beyond the trickling water, further steps lead to a grave believed to be that of his wife. Sheikh Noorul was sent to the Cape in the 17th century, during which time he spent a period on Robben Island, along with other religious and political exiles.

According to legend he escaped from the island – by what means is open to dispute – and hid out on this spot on the mountain. Under cover of darkness he made contact and remained in touch with slaves living on local estates, over time teaching them from the Qur'an and in this way becoming the local *imam*. Today, some claim to see a spirit on horseback at noon, riding over the waves from Robben Island, on its way to take lessons from the *imam* at the *kramat*. Further along Victoria Road, nearer to Bakoven is another, lesser-known shrine to Sayed Jaffer.

Interior of Sheikh Noorul Mubeen's kramat

Sheikh Abdurahman Matebe's kramat *in Constantia*

Sheikh Noorul Mubeen's kramat *in Oudekraal*

Constantia

Sweeping around the mountain via Llandudno and Hout Bay to Constantia, several important Muslim shrines lie along the Spaanschemat River Road/M42, bordering onto the vineyards of Buitenverwachting, Klein Constantia and Constantia Uitsig. The most prominent

Interior of Sheikh Sayed Mahmud's kramat

Sheikh Sayed Mahmud's kramat *on Islam Hill in Constantia*

Plaque commemorating prisoners on the Polsbroek

is the grave of Sheikh Abdurahman Matebe Shah, who originally arrived at the Cape from Batavia (Jakarta, northwest Java) on 13 May 1668 on board the *Polsbroek*. He was previously a Malaccan sultan, regarded as an *orang cayen* – meaning 'a man of power and influence'.

Malacca was the centre of trade and military power on the Malaysian peninsula, and resisted Portuguese rule. However, the entire Malaccan empire was gradually overrun by the Portuguese, and by 1511, only the city of Malacca and certain Sumatran strongholds were able to withstand their rule. Subsequently, the Dutch, in 1667, attacked and captured the Malaccan fortress of Soeroesang. Executing the sultan would have been tantamount to turning him into a holy martyr, so he was banished to the Cape Colony.

Oral history recounts how he befriended and taught the slaves in Constantia. We have no exact date for his death – estimated between 1682 and 1685 – but he was buried at the gateway to Klein Constantia. A simple wooden shack subsequently commemorated the spot. Over time this structure became dilapidated and The Cape Mazaar (Kramat) Society replaced it with a new building, designed by acclaimed Cape Town architect Gawie Fagan.

Another prisoner carrying *orang cayen* status who arrived at the Cape on board the *Polsbroek* was Sayed Mahmud, one of the main religious and spiritual leaders in Malacca. He joined Sheikh Abdurahman in teaching Islam practices to the slaves of Constantia. His shrine is on top of a small hillock called Islam Hill, a short walk from Summit Road on Groot Constantia's wine estate. Other shrines to scholars such as Sheikh Abdul Mutalib may be found within Constantia forest.

False Bay

On towards the False Bay coastline, at Faure, you will find the *kramat* of Sheikh Yusuf on the farm Zandvliet. Sheikh Yusuf is renowned as one of the foremost Islamic religious leaders at the Cape (see Fact File on his life on page 61) and the beautiful *kramat* erected in his memory is a site of pilgrimage for many Cape Muslims today.

Robben Island

It is appropriate that we come full circle on Robben Island, with the *kramat* to Tuan Matarah, since many religious captives spent time here. Tuan Matarah, also known as Sayed Abdurahman Motura, was revered as a great spiritual teacher and healer. Legends passed down through generations claim that his powers extended to being able to walk over the water from Robben Island to Cape Town! His *kramat* was constructed in the 1960s by the apartheid prison authorities.

Women praying in the kramat *of Tuan Matarah on Robben Island*

An Early History of Bo-Kaap Mosques

On Religion

And an old priest said, Speak to us of Religion.
And he said:
Have I spoken this day of aught else?
Is religion all deeds and all reflection,
And that which is neither deed nor reflection,
but a wonder and a surprise ever springing in
the soul, even while the hands hew the stone
or tend the loom?
Who can separate his faith from his actions,
or his belief from his occupations?
Who can spread his hours before him, saying
'This for God and this for myself; This for my
soul and this other for my body'?
All your hours are wings that beat through
space from self to self to self.
He who wears his morality but as his best
garment were better naked.
The wind and the sun will tear no holes in his skin.
And he who defines his conduct by ethics imprisons
his song-bird in a cage.
The freest song comes not through bars and wires.
And he to whom worshipping is a window,
to open but also to shut, has not yet visited the house
of his soul whose windows are from dawn to dawn.

Source: The Prophet *by Kahlil Gibran*

The mosque and its origins

he word 'mosque' derives from the Arabic *masjid*, meaning 'place of prayer'. In the Bo-Kaap, the mosque acts as the centre of the community, for both religious as well as secular activities. Tucked into the narrow streets, these mosques offer examples of some of the oldest architecture to have survived from the time of the emancipation of slaves. There are at least 10 mosques within the original demarcation of the Bo-Kaap, making this the most densely packed sector of Islamic religious buildings in South Africa.

The first mosque to be built was conceptualised around the courtyard architecture of the Prophet Muhammad's house in Medina, constructed after he completed his journey from Mecca to Medina in 622CE. This is where Muhammad knelt to pray, and his followers came to view it as sacred ground. Since then, throughout history, and also dependent on local architectural styles, the mosque has undergone change. However it remains essentially an open space, generally covered with a roof, for prayer.

Inside the mosque, an area with running water is provided so that followers may wash prior to prayer. At the front of the prayer area a semicircular niche, called the *mihrab*, which faces towards Mecca and is reserved for the prayer leader, or *imam*. To the right of the *mihrab*, at the top of steps, is a seat called the *minbar*, used as a pulpit by the preacher (*khatib*). The minaret (*ma'dhanah*) is where the muezzin (*mu'adhdhin*) calls the faithful to worship five times a day. Originally, this was simply a raised position above the mosque, but it has become a 'prayer tower'.

Mosques provide a vital link with Islam and the past, and the following early history, from information gathered mainly from the work of renowned historian Achmat Davids, offers us fascinating insight to their development up to the 19th century.

An early photograph of the khatib *and* imams *next to the* minbar

Auwal Mosque, on Dorp Street, the oldest mosque in South Africa

Auwal Mosque, Dorp Street

Built in 1798, this is South Africa's oldest mosque and was the country's first formal centre of worship, education and dissemination of Islamic culture. Imam Abdullah *Kadi* Abdus Salaam – or Tuan Guru (see page 13) – was its first *imam*. Incarcerated on Robben Island between 1780 and 1793, he became active in the Muslim community on his release.

On 26 September 1794, a freed Muslim slave, Coridon van Ceylon, purchased two properties in Dorp Street. (Slaves were named according to their country of origin; hence, Coridon was 'from Ceylon'.) On his death three years later, these properties passed to his son-in-law Achmat van Bengalen, originally from Chinsura in Bengal. Achmat was a student of Tuan Guru, and was happy to make one of these properties available to him to use as a mosque. Tuan Guru appointed a man by the name of Rijaap as his second in command, in the hope that he would succeed him as *imam* but Rijaap died before he could take up the position. When Tuan Guru died in 1807, the Imamship went to Abdulalim, who was instructed by Tuan Guru on his deathbed:

'Achmat van Bengalen shall be your second priest and will assist you in the performance of your duties.'

The appointment of Abdulalim caused much dissent in the Muslim community. Frans van Bengalen, who led the Javanese Artillery at the Battle of Blaauwberg, requested that, instead, a Jan van Boughies be made *imam*. Achmat van Bengalen refused, at which Frans and Jan resigned from the Auwal Mosque. They started their own congregation in Long Street, and this became the famous Palm Tree Mosque.

Achmat van Bengalen was appointed *kadi*, or spiritual head of the community. In terms of Islamic law, the *kadi* need not also be the *imam* of the mosque, but he is responsible for Islamic education of the community. Achmat's concession offering all slaves who embraced Islam their immediate freedom made sure there were many converts to the faith – to such an extent that the Earl of Caledon, who preceded Sir John Cradock as governor at the Cape, expressed the concern that 'if the slaves were left in a state of ignorance, they would fall prey to the zeal of the *imams* who were conducting a school in Cape Town'. In 1825 Achmat recorded 491 free black and slave children in attendance.

Achmat van Bengalen eventually became *imam* of the mosque in 1822. He died at 42 Dorp Street a year later, on 9 October, aged 93. On his death notice he was acknowledged as the 'high priest of the Malays'.

The Auwal Mosque has been much altered and only two walls of the original structure remain. In 1930 major alterations were necessary when part of the building collapsed; the prayer minaret was added around this time. The mosque's loyal Shafee school of thought accounts for over 90 per cent of the Bo-Kaap's Muslim community. Many of the Muslim religious traditions unique to the Cape must have originated here – for example, *rampie-sny*, the cutting of orange leaves on the Prophet's birthday.

The minbar *and* mihrab *inside the Auwal Mosque*

Caretaker at the entrance to the mosque

Palm Tree Mosque, Long Street

This mosque – the second oldest in South Africa – actually started as a *langgar* (Indonesian for 'prayer room') in the upper storey of Jan van Boughies' house. It was only granted mosque status in 1825 by Achmat van Bengalen.

From the beginning, things did not run smoothly here in Long Street. Achmat once commented that Jan had 'a troublesome nature', and within a year most of his congregation, including the *imam*, Adolgamiet, had returned to the Auwal Mosque. Frans van Bengalen also tired of Jan and returned to Batavia, leaving Jan to run his beleaguered assembly on his own. Infighting continued between Achmat van Bengalen and Jan van Boughies, prompting Jan to publish the following letter on 13 February 1836 in the *South African Commercial Advertiser*:

> **Beloved Countrymen and Fellow Mohammedans!**
> *Having seen and read a printed document in which ACHMAT himself declares that he was appointed Imam by Prince Abdullah. This is untrue. I as the oldest Priest who have been in the religious service of the Moham-medan religion for the last 38 years know nothing about this. Thus my congregation and myself do not recognise him as a Priest. There was never a Prince Abdullah at the Cape of Good Hope, though there was an Imam Abdullah or Chief Priest.*

The famous palm tree in front of the Palm Tree Mosque

The minbar *and* mihrab *inside Palm Tree Mosque*

I, as the oldest schoolteacher in the Mohammedan language gave Achmat lessons. This I can prove. I further wish to express my thanks to the Government and Officials for the many years of goodwill.

Signed: Asnoun, Eldest Priest
Under the name of Jan van Boughies
Church No. 32 Long Street

Jan van Boughies' life story is a colourful one. He had arrived in Cape Town during the later part of the 1700s as a slave from the southwestern region of the Celebes, known as Bughies. Salia van Macassar, a freed slave as her name suggests, bought Jan van Boughies – but fell in love with her 'purchase', and they were married according to Muslim custom. When Jan was in his fifties, Salia died and he took a new wife; Sameda van de Kaap was a freed slave barely 15 years old. By this time Jan was extremely wealthy, and was able to purchase many slaves – whom he then set free. He died on 12 November 1846, an incredible 112 years old.

Although it started as the Jan van Boughies Mosque, it was renamed the Palm Tree Mosque in the late 1970s, inspired by the two palms standing in front of it – purportedly planted by Jan himself.

Entrance to the Palm Tree Mosque

The unusual frontage of the Nurul Islam Mosque

Nurul Islam Mosque, Buitengracht Street

The third mosque in South Africa, this was founded in 1834 by Imam Abdol Rauf, Tuan Guru's younger son. Originally, a stream flowed next to the mosque, which was used for washing before prayers. The Nurul Islam Mosque on Buitengracht is the first to have been founded by an entire congregation.

Abdol Rauf and his older brother, Abdol Rakiep, had been placed under the guardianship of Achmat van Bengalen. Rakiep led the Mohammedan Shafee congregation till his death in 1834, after which Rauf took over. At first they met in private houses, as the mosque was only acquired on 27 February 1844. Abdol Rauf was an exceptionally competent *imam* and served his community for 25 years, assisted by Achmat's sons Mochamat, Hamien and Saddik.

Abdol Rauf was also a charismatic influence in the Muslim community. He was very active with a group in Claremont, where a wealthy resident had donated land on the Main Road in 1854. Here, the first Claremont mosque was built, with Abdol Rauf as the *imam* and trustee. He remained *imam* of both mosques until his death in 1859.

Abdul van Bengalen's son, Hamien, took over at the Nurul Islam mosque. He was also the guardian of Abdol Rauf's three youngest sons, and one of them, Abdol Rakiep, was elected *imam* upon his guardian's death in 1867. Abdol Rakiep was barely 20, but was already very knowledgeable in Islamic practice. His lack of experience, however, led him to make some controversial decisions. He immediately made changes to Friday worship.

The mosque, by virtue of its name, practised Islam in accordance with the Shafee school of thought which stipulated that Friday congregational, or *Jumu'ah*, prayers could only be performed if 40 or more worshippers were present. This was often not the case, though, and it meant that *Jumu'ah* prayers could not proceed; they were then replaced by ordinary midday prayers. This infuriated Abdol Rakiep, so he decided to perform the *Jumu'ah* in terms of Hanafee beliefs, which set down a minimum of three worshippers. The result was great confrontation with the congregation – at one point Abdol was forced, for his own protection, to call in the police during the Friday *Jumu'ah* prayers.

As *imam*, Abdol Rakiep was sued for malpractice in 1873, with the case going to the Supreme Court. Abdol ultimately won, but it was the start of a bitter feud between the Hanafee and Shafee schools, which continued until the 1920s.

It is relevant to observe that there are four major jurisprudential schools of thought within the religion of Islam, including those of Hanafee and Shafee Muslims. They differ only with respect to minor interpretations of the Qur'an and the Hadith (the Prophet's words), and the Muslim scholars who developed these schools of thought bore no hostility towards each other. Today, fortunately, adherents to Hanafee and Shafee beliefs exist in harmony within the Bo-Kaap.

Jamia / Queen Victoria Mosque, corner Chiappini Street and Hout Lane

This mosque is adjacent to the disused stone quarry in Chiappini Street. The Jamia, or Queen Victoria, mosque as it is also known to honour the land grant and patronage of the British Crown, is the largest in the Bo-Kaap. In the 1790s, the first Friday congregational prayers (*Jumu'ah*) were read here, making it the fifth oldest mosque in South Africa.

It was the first Shafee mosque to be built on land specifically set aside for that purpose, from a land grant that arose out of social and political conflicts in the Cape Colony in 1846. Confrontation was increasing on the 'eastern

View of Jamia/Queen Victoria Mosque

77

An early photograph of the Queen Victoria Mosque

Women reciting the Qur'an

frontier', and maintaining the loyalty of the Cape residents became a crucial issue. Muslims comprised a healthy one-third of the total population and in an effort to curry their favour, they were promised a mosque. On 22 April 1846, the worsening situation on the eastern front led to martial law being declared in the Cape. A week later a declaration issued by Governor Montagu made it a criminal offence not to enrol for military duty. In May of that year all males between the ages of 16 and 60 living within the municipality of Cape Town and Green Point were conscripted.

The Malay Corps arrived in Grahamstown on 23 May 1846, consisting of 250 Muslim conscripts. Their commanding officer, Dr Munro, described them as 'sturdy-looking fellows … dressed rather picturesquely in dark blue, with large red cotton handkerchiefs folded like turbans round their heads. The Malays marched along merrily and seemed daily to acquire a more martial bearing and appearance.' Despondency soon filled the ranks, though, when it was clear that the military administration had broken their agreement to supply food to the families left at the Cape.

The Malay Corps remained on the eastern frontier until 16 September 1846, when they were demobilised by General Cloete. On arrival back in Cape Town they pressed for their mosque site, ultimately granted on 19 October 1851, with the deeds of transfer finalised three years later.

One early report on the mosque in 1862 described it thus:

A large room, like a country ballroom, with glass chandeliers, carpeted with common carpet, all but a space at the entrance, railed off for shoes; the Caaba and the pulpit at one end; over the niche, a crescent painted; and over the entrance door a crescent, an Arabic inscription, and the royal arms of England!

Little is known about the first *imam*, Abdol Bazier, and his son, Abdol Wahab, succeeded him. Abdol Wahab's greatest contribution to the Cape Muslim community was the acquisition of the Faure *kramat* camping ground and the construction of Sheikh Yusuf's shrine. Although there is no definitive proof that Sheikh Yusuf's remains lie there, Abdol felt the shrine would serve to unite the Muslim community.

Mosque Shafee, Chiappini Street

To the eyes of visitors, Chiappini Street is the most tangible of the Bo-Kaap landmarks. The mosque situated here developed out of two separate congregations that existed side by side. Imam Hadjie initially acquired a plot of land between Helliger Lane and Church Street in September 1859, and began constructing a mosque, but he died on a pilgrimage to Mecca in 1869. Imam Tajieb obtained a second adjacent plot in May 1876, and work began on this mosque. The congregations eventually amalgamated, the two pieces of land were consolidated and one mosque was built. It was referred to as the Mosque of Imam Hadjie but its name was later changed to Mosque Shafee. Imam Tajieb became the head of the unified congregation, and he was eventually succeeded by Imam Abdol Kariem.

Imam Abdol Kariem's close ties with government officials played a huge role in the 1883–86 dispute over the Tana Baru (see pages 10–15), which culminated in him being arrested and charged with contravening the Public Health Act; the charges were subsequently withdrawn.

After Abdol Kariem died in 1889, the mosque went through a rather turbulent period in its history. Abdol Gasiep, as successor, came into conflict with his congregation and ended up in the Cape Supreme Court. He appears to have confined his duties to minor religious services, relying on his assistants, among them Sheikh Abdol Azzizi, to carry out most of the work. Sheikh Abdol, a native of Mecca, was a learned Islam scholar who became increasingly popular with the congregation and threatened Kariem's position as *imam*. In 1991 the *imam* sued the sheikh, along with his supporters.

In his judgement of the case, Chief Justice Buchanan declared that the laws of the Muslim community were very vague and that it was difficult for the court to determine the rights of the parties involved. In his summation,

he felt the conflict had developed as a clash between the old and new order of Islam at the Cape. The 'new order' he attributed to an increasing number of pilgrims having gone to Mecca, studied there and returned more knowledgeable than those who had remained behind.

The Chief Justice, however, seems to have confused this case with the *Hanafee vs. Shafee* dispute, which had little relation to the case. The Hanafee school (or 'new order' to which the Chief Justice was referring) had already become popular in Cape Town 30 years earlier with the arrival of Abubakr Effendi.

A much more constructive phase in the history of this mosque took place under the Imamship of Sheikh Achmat Behardien – acknowledged as one of the most charismatic sheikhs in Cape Town in the 20th century. Trained in Saudi Arabia and one of the founder members of the Muslim Judicial Council, he was life president until his death in 1973. Sheikh Achmat was the main spokesman for the Cape Muslim community during the years 1945–66.

Masjied Boorhaanol Islam / Pilgrim Mosque, Longmarket Street

This and the following Nurul Mohamadia Mosque in Vos Street were offshoots of the Jamia / Queen Victoria mosque. The health of Jamia Mosque's *imam*, Shahibo, began to deteriorate in 1881. Wanting his son to take over the position, Shahibo got him to take over many of his duties, but members of the congregation did not believe this to be the correct choice. Matters came to a head in 1884 when mosque officials could no longer tolerate the situation; they left to form a separate congregation at 31 Chiappini Street, and instigated legal action to try to remove Shahibo as *imam*. An unpleasant legal battle ensued. In the meantime, the breakaway group started building a mosque in Longmarket Street – known originally as the Pilgrim Mosque.

Hadjie Abdol Kaliel was the first *imam* of the Pilgrim congregation. A few weeks before his death in July 1898, he adopted Mavia Davids, who would become the father of noted historian Achmat Davids. Mavia graduated from his Qur'an studies at age eight, and his *tamat* was the first to be performed at the Pilgrim Mosque.

When legal struggles arose at the mosque over matters of religious protocol, a period of calm was ushered in with the arrival of Imam Abdol Bassier, who proved to be both competent and an efficient administrator. He also became involved in the broader activities of the Cape Muslim community.

Masjied Boorhaanol Islam Mosque, circa 1900

The mosque became dilapidated over time and was one of a group of properties affected by the Slums Act proclamation in 1934. The City Council wanted to move the congregation to an alternative mosque site, but after heated debate the congregation rejected this.

Pilgrim Mosque featured the first prayer minaret constructed in Cape Town. Unfortunately in the late 1930s it blew off in a storm. When it was replaced, the new minaret looked so out of place, it was decided that the entire mosque needed renovating. At the same time, an application was submitted to the Registrar of Deeds to change the mosque's name to Boorhaanol Islam. This was granted in 1949. The mosque was declared a national monument in 1966 and in 1970 its name was again changed, to the Masjied Boorhaanol Islam. Many community-oriented projects were run from here, and today the Boorhaanol Recreational Movement based here acts as the area's main social welfare group.

Nurul Mohamadia Mosque, Vos Street

In the 1890s, tension flared once again at the Jamia Mosque. The congregation was dissatisfied with the way the finances of the mosque were being administered by Imam Shahibo's son, Hadjie Hassiem. The annoyed members claimed Hadjie was using the next- door buildings, erected for catering purposes on Muslim feast days, as his personal residence and to house his cows! The disagreement turned nasty, with Hadjie calling his detractors 'pigs' and 'dogs' who needed to be thrown out of the mosque. The mosque, in the meanwhile, became more rundown with no money being spent to restore it, so Hadjie Salie Jacob and other members of the congregation went to court to settle their dispute. However, they received no satisfaction through the legal system and Hadjie Salie Jacob and the other dissident members of the congregation withdrew from the Jamia Mosque to form the Nurul Mohamadia congregation.

The transfer of deeds for the land on which the mosque now stands took place on 29 December 1899. To avoid a repeat confrontation as had occurred at Jamia, the deeds stated that there should be a register of members who alone would have voting powers, and that these trustees would be required to keep the register up to date to 'avoid in the future unseemly disputes'. The members were also to have the power to vote for the election of the *imam* or 'upon matters affecting the said building or said congregation'. A further condition stipulated that the building would not be open to public worship on Fridays, to avoid compounding the dispute already raging at the time over the Shafee *Jumu'ah*. Yet another condition of the deed was the power vested with the *imam* to appoint office bearers.

Thus, the Nurul Mohamadia Mosque was the first in the Bo-Kaap to have a proper constitution that defined the rights of the *imam* and the members. This firm organisational foundation resulted in it being the only 19th-century mosque in the Bo-Kaap to not have become embroiled in Supreme Court litigations.

It was Hadjie Salie Jacob's son, Gatiep Ebrahem Salie, who became *imam*, and he served until October 1928, when the Imamship passed on to his son.

Jamia (Hanafee) Mosque, corner Long Street and Dorp Street

This is one of two Hanafee mosques serving the Bo-Kaap community (the other is the Quawatul Islam Mosque). Both were constructed after the Hanafee code was first introduced to the Cape Colony, giving rise to intense conflict between the Shafee and Hanafee religious schools of thought – or the so-called 'old' and 'new' orders.

Abubakr Effendi, who came to the Cape in 1863, was held in high esteem by the Hanafee Muslim community and acted as one of their first religious teachers. The mosque was dedicated to his memory, although its first *imam* was Achmat Sedick.

Abubakr Effendi's sons, most notably Achmat, were involved in the construction of the mosque and played an important role in establishing the Moslem Cemetery Board. During the Tana Baru dispute, Achmat united the Hanafee and Shafee schools. He served on major delegation committees with the premier, governor and the colonial secretary, and later announced his intention to stand for a seat in the Cape Parliament.

As the first Muslim to stand for a position, the Cape Government wanted to make sure he would not be elected, but Cecil John Rhodes, Paul Sauer and Jan Hofmeyer were too politically shrewd to involve government in legislation that could be seen to be tampering with the constitution. Besides, they didn't want to alienate the Cape Muslim community who by now comprised a sizable proportion of the electorate. Instead, a private members' bill was brought before Parliament to curtail the cumulative vote in Cape Town – as this vote would most probably have seen Effendi gaining a seat. Despite political wrangling, the bill became law; Achmat Effendi ultimately lost out, failing to receive the required number of votes to gain his seat in Parliament.

In the early 1900s Ismail 'Ma-awia' Mania became *imam* of the Jamia Mosque. He had trained in Mecca, becoming a *hafiz* – a person who recites the entire Qur'an from memory. A brilliant scholar, Ismail received a gold medal for reciting the Holy Qur'an at Mecca's Grand Mosque. During his time as *imam*, he established a Muslim school, or *madrassah* (also *madressa*), at the mosque, teaching extensively in both the Shafee and Hanafee traditions. Of interest is that, by presenting both schools of thought, he did much to diffuse the antagonism between the two groups.

This mosque is still highly respected for the teaching that students receive, and the level of knowledge of the *tamats*, or *grandaunts*, at the school.

Quawatul Islam Mosque, Loop Street

The building of this mosque in 1892 was the result of the influx of Mauritian and Indian Muslims to the Cape Colony during the latter part of the 19th century. It was the first Hanafee mosque founded in the Bo-Kaap, as they found it difficult to integrate into the Shafee mosques already established there.

The Quawatul Islam Mosque had a board of trustees who were duly empowered to appoint or dismiss the *imam*. The initial deed document reads:

> *The trustees or the majority of them for the time being shall have the absolute power to appoint the Imam to officiate in the aforesaid mosque for such term as to them shall seem necessary, and to impose on him and his successors such conditions in writing as shall be necessary for the due and proper discharge of his office and for his good, moral and proper behaviour in accordance with the laws of the Qur'an and the recognised customs of the Indian Sect worshipping in the said mosque and the said trustees either unanimously or by majority shall have the power either to remove or to suspend the said Imam from office for any breach of his contract.*

The first *imam* thus appointed was Mogamat Taliep, then the leading authority on Islamic law at the Cape. He had studied in both Mauritius and Bombay, and could speak Urdu fluently. Most of the newly established congregation were unable to speak English or Afrikaans, and racial conflict arose between them and the established Muslim community as a result.

The new settlers began to express their cultural superiority by not permitting their daughters to marry into the settled community. In retaliation, the established Bo-Kaap community referred to them as *babis* – an Indonesian word for 'pigs'. Imam Taliep, who was greatly respected by the Cape Town communities and the authorities alike, did much to diffuse this racial strife. However, tension persisted until 1948, when the government forced the two groups to seek accord and abandon their racial clashes. A growing band of young Muslim intellectuals within the Quawatul Islam Mosque took up the lead to establish unity; to them, such racial tension was contrary to the teachings of Islam and was, in fact, threatening their religion. Out of this group grew the Muslim Teachers' Association, in 1951, and later, in 1958, the Muslim Youth League.

Although the Quawatul Islam Mosque was initially established to serve the Indian Muslim community, it eventually, with time and integration, came to serve the entire Bo-Kaap community. According to author Achmat Davids, this mosque 'is important in the history of the Cape Muslim community, as it shows the cohesive power of Islam to draw different cultural groups, even against their wishes, into a common brotherhood'.

Leeuwen Street Mosque (Nural Huda Mosque), Upper Leeuwen Street

Any description of the mosques of the Bo-Kaap would be incomplete without a brief mention of the mosque in Upper Leeuwen Street. This is a relative newcomer to the area, built in Schoone Kloof and completed in 1958. The style of architecture is much more modern than the other mosques described. The aerial photograph gives a good indication of how the mosque is placed within the centre of the CBD.

Achmat Davids
Islamic historian of the Bo-Kaap

Achmat Davids, lovingly known as 'Apatjie' (referring to his fatherly role) was born on 11 May 1939. He was the youngest son in a family of five sisters and three brothers, all living at 203 Longmarket Street in the Bo-Kaap. As a child, Achmat found school history lessons intensely boring. Ironic, then, that he went on to become a 'walking encyclopaedia' on all matters related to the Bo-Kaap.

It was in fulfilling the social needs of his community within the Bo-Kaap that he found his calling. As a wonderfully insightful social worker (with a diploma in the Social Sciences, UCT, 1964), he galvanised people into reflecting on their existence under apartheid; he was also the only, solitary, Muslim spokesperson on socioeconomic issues in the days of *The Cape Herald* newspaper. As a founder member of the Muslim Assembly in 1969, he challenged and transcended the narrowly defined world of the sanctimoniously religious.

Achmat's involvement at a community level led him to establish preschool education, Boy Scout and Brownie troupes, religious education workshops, soup kitchens for the destitute and the renovation of a rundown community centre in the Bo-Kaap. He was a champion of the people and fondly reminded his students: 'You cannot be an educator without a social conscience.'

During the 1970s and 1980s, Achmat spent much of his time promoting the need for education among preschool children. He served as vice-chairman of the Western Cape Association for Early Childhood Education (1978–84); and vice-chairman/member of the Board of Management for the Sallie Davies Training College for pre-primary teachers (1983–87). He was also the founding member of many local welfare organisations.

KEEPING THE CAPE MUSLIM FIRE BURNING

Achmat was perpetually interested in researching the history of the Muslims in South Africa. In 1991, he completed a Masters thesis with honours at the University of Natal on 'The Afrikaans of Cape Muslims from 1815 to 1915'. His theory was that the Afrikaans language originated in the Bo-Kaap among the slave people living there. It was a language known then as 'Kitchen Dutch' as it used to be spoken in the kitchens of the slaves' wealthy masters. Achmat went on to suggest that if the British had not conquered the Cape, the Afrikaners would not have adopted the language.

The following years, 1992 and 1993, he was awarded fellowships to Yale University in the USA. Accolades followed in the form of an honorary doctorate from the Sheikh Yusuf Islamic University in

Indonesia, in recognition of his research into early Islamic history at the Cape. He went on to give extensive lecture tours on his work in Holland, Indonesia and Malaysia.

Achmat wrote several major books about Islam at the Cape, including:

~ *Mosques of the Bo-Kaap* (1980)
~ *The History of the Tana Baru* (1985)
~ *Pages from Cape Muslim History* (co-editor, 1994)

For him, history was not about the past but about the present. This was most obvious in his struggle for the preservation of Oudekraal and the restoration of the Tana Baru – the first Muslim graveyard on the slopes of Signal Hill. During 1994 Achmat played a leading role in the tricentenary celebrations of Islam in Cape Town.

Imam Abdurahmaan Bassier has described him as a '*mensch*' – an extraordinarily loving human being. 'No-one can claim that they ever came to Achmat Davids for anything and that they left empty-handed. Achmat relished giving of his time, his expertise, his money – whatever little he had, literally of his self.'

He eventually became a presenter and later station manager of the Voice of the Cape radio programme. In this capacity, he hosted hundreds of talk shows, seeking to be a voice for Muslims who were comfortable with the challenge of coexistence, intra-religious tolerance and an all-embracing 'South Africanness'.

Achmat Davids' life was cut short by a heart attack on 15 September 1998. Literally thousands of mourners lined Longmarket, Rose and Chiappini streets to pay their last respects to 'the Doc', or 'Boeta Achmat'. These included leading historians, *imams*, sheikhs, government officials and the people of the Bo-Kaap for whom he had done so much during his lifetime.

In 2000 Achmat Davids' name was recorded in the City of Cape Town Civic Honours Book in recognition of his work as a historian and humanitarian. In remembrance of this admirable human being, the following are some of the tributes that poured in after he passed away.

He was the unofficial mayor of the Bo-Kaap, whom everyone knew. He was not afraid to explore the legacy of Islam. A pioneer in linguistics, especially the Afrikaans language, he lived for the community and died while serving the community.

Shafieq Morton, Voice of the Cape editor

Achmat was an extraordinary historian – he was always close to the people. He loved them and took a keen interest in them and I think he will always be remembered as 'the historian of Bo-Kaap'.

Dullah Omar (1939–2004), former Minister of Justice

Achmat Davids and friends

Cultural Expression in Song and Art

⤜⧬⤛

Daar kom die Alibama

⤜⧬⤛

Afrikaans	*English*
Daar kom die Alibama,	*There comes the Alibama,*
Die Alibama kom oor die see,	*The Alibama comes over the sea,*
Daar kom die Alibama,	*There comes the Alibama,*
Die Alibama kom oor die see.	*The Alibama comes over the sea.*
Nooi, Nooi, die rietkooi nooi,	*Girl, girl, the reed bed girl,*
Die rietkooi is gemaak,	*The reed bed is made,*
Die rietkooi is vir my gemaak	*The reed bed is made*
Om daar op te slaap.	*For me to sleep on.*
Nooi, Nooi, die rietkooi nooi,	*Girl, girl, the reed bed is made,*
Die rietkooi is gemaak,	*The reed bed is made,*
Die rietkooi is vir my gemaak	*The reed bed is made*
Om daar op te slaap.	*For me to sleep on.*
O Alibama, die Alibama,	*Oh, Alibama, the Alibama,*
O Alibama, kom oor die see,	*Oh, Alibama, come over the sea,*
O Alibama, die Alibama,	*Oh, Alibama, the Alibama,*
O Alibama, kom oor die see.	*Oh, Alibama, come over the sea.*

Recording history through song

he song *Daar kom die Alibama* is one of many that have survived from the time of the Dutch East India Company. They are the result of a rich cross-pollination of lifestyles, culture, language and music that took place between the Malay slaves, indigenous peoples of the Cape, the Dutch and other European settlers. Two stories exist around this particular song's origin. The first, and most likely, is that it was composed about the US Confederate raiding ship, *Alabama*, which called in at Cape Town in 1863 during the American Civil War, after capturing the Federal ship, *Sea Bride*, in Table Bay. A huge party was held on the beach, where the captain, Admiral Semmes, handed out provisions seized during the raid. The second theory is that there was a local boat called *Alabama*, which brought thatching reeds to Cape Town from St Helena Bay, on the West Coast. Either way, it was a popular song of the time and is still sung by many Coon Carnival troops (see page 99) today.

GHOEMA – THE ORIGIN OF MUSICAL CULTURE

In 2005, to celebrate the unique musical traditions of the Cape, the renowned duo, David Kramer and Taliep Petersen, created a musical review entitled *Ghoema*. It was the latest endeavour of these icons of the South African music and theatre industry. Their musical delves deep into early South African history at the Cape, exploring the roots of slave music back to the era of the Dutch East India Company. Since the late 1980s works by this duo, among them *District Six*, *Fairyland*, *Crooners*, *Poison*, *Klop Klop* and *Kat And The Kings*, have played internationally, winning major awards on both Broadway and London's West End.

The word *ghoema* denotes a drum made from a small wooden barrel or vat, from which the lid and base have been removed and an animal skin stretched tightly over one end. It's small enough to be carried and played while walking. The drum may have originated in either Zanzibar or Madagascar, since in these countries the Swahili word for drum is *ngoma*. The *ghoema* plays a significant role in the traditional music of the Cape Malay people.

In David Kramer's words, 'Slavery played an enormous role in the creation and evolution of Cape culture and its music. Slaves, imported by the Dutch from various countries, brought with them their cultures. Their cultures interacted with the culture of the European settlers. This resulted in the evolution of a specific type of culture and music – *ghoema* music.'

Taliep Petersen, musical director of the show of the same name, explains: 'You can compare the birth of *ghoema* music in the Cape with the creation of blues in the United States, or the samba in Latin America, or Creole music in the Caribbean. All these types of music have one thing in common: slavery.'

A CLASSIC DUTCH FOLK SONG

Another song that has survived across the years, *Rosa*, tells of a love affair in the slave community, when a young man expresses his feelings and proposes; after three months they meet again and set a wedding date. This song is still very popular within the community and is frequently sung at weddings.

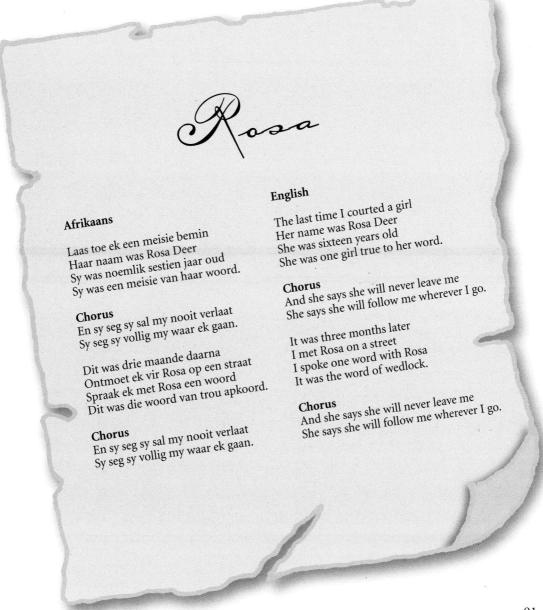

Rosa

Afrikaans

Laas toe ek een meisie bemin
Haar naam was Rosa Deer
Sy was noemlik sestien jaar oud
Sy was een meisie van haar woord.

Chorus
En sy seg sy sal my nooit verlaat
Sy seg sy vollig my waar ek gaan.

Dit was drie maande daarna
Ontmoet ek vir Rosa op een straat
Spraak ek met Rosa een woord
Dit was die woord van trou apkoord.

Chorus
En sy seg sy sal my nooit verlaat
Sy seg sy vollig my waar ek gaan.

English

The last time I courted a girl
Her name was Rosa Deer
She was sixteen years old
She was one girl true to her word.

Chorus
And she says she will never leave me
She says she will follow me wherever I go.

It was three months later
I met Rosa on a street
I spoke one word with Rosa
It was the word of wedlock.

Chorus
And she says she will never leave me
She says she will follow me wherever I go.

TRADITIONAL SONG TYPES

Ghoemaliedjies (picnic songs)

Also called *ghommaliedjies*, these songs are sung on outings such as picnics; they are often also called *afklop* or *piekniekliedjies*. They originated among the slaves and usually have a satirical element, employing a system of coded words to describe the relationship between slave and owner. In many cases, the songs are laced with sexual innuendos. Sung to the lively rhythm of the *ghoema* drum, they consist of short refrains joined together in what is termed *vyf-aan-die-bos*.

Moppies (comic songs)

Moppies and *ghoemaliedjies* are so similar in style they are often confused. The roots of *moppies*, which are comic songs, lie in the Dutch *straatliederen* (or street songs). They usually have a storyline running through them, differentiating these songs from the juxtapositional format of the *ghoemaliedjie*.

The Tulips performing Nederlandseliedjies *in the mid-1980s*

Krontjong

This folk music from Indonesia is a meshing of different styles and elements from divergent cultures, originating among a specific subgroup of Eurasians. These people had a complex ethnic background created of crewmen and slaves who arrived on trading vessels throughout the 16th century. *Krontjong* is also the name of a five-stringed ukulele-like instrument, integral to the playing of this type of music.

Nederlandseliedjies (Dutch folk songs)

Most of these are believed to be several hundred years old, and relate historical events, such as the Battle of Waterloo. Other songs are local hybrids, most of them created and collected in the 19th century. *Rosa* is a very good example.

Many of the songs would have been sung on board the slave galleys transporting their human cargo to the Cape. It is easy to imagine the *ghoema* beating out the rhythm as the slaves rowed, attempting to keep up their spirits with song. On other ships, acapella choirs were organised to give the slaves a sense of unity.

Songs were also a way of keeping up to date with current events. In Cape Town, the lamplighter would leave from the Slave Lodge, having picked up information from the slaves. As he lit the gas street lamps, he would disperse the information in songs sung in his native language so that the Dutch masters were none the wiser. Thus, many of the songs had strong political and social overtones. A line from one of these songs goes: 'On the eleventh of this month, when the full moon is here, we will go marching!'

The Goodhope Entertainers in the mid-1990s

93

MALAY MUSIC EVOLVES

After the abolition of slavery, song within the community developed in two very distinct ways: the Malay choirs (which originated in the *nagtroepe*, or 'night minstrels', and Christmas choirs) and the Coon troupes.

Nagtroepe

On New Year's Eve, 1887, a Malay choir formed a torchlight procession, going from tavern to tavern in Cape Town to entertain the merrymakers with choral songs. This type of choir came to be known as *nagtroepe*, and eventually became a regular part of New Year celebrations in the Bo-Kaap.

One of the singers of the very first group was 20-year-old Rasdien Cornelis who, along with his assistant Sulaiman, used to row out to the Dutch boats that came into Cape Town harbour, taking fresh supplies to them. In exchange, the seamen would sing them *Nederlandseliedjes*, which they copied down and then incorporated into their minstrel repertoire. It is due to their efforts that many of these songs are still sung today.

Modern minstrels tend to dress in a tracksuit with a cap and cane, and walk through the streets with a comic dance step, collecting money as they go. A variety of instruments, including banjo, guitar, violin, mandolin and the *ghoema*, are used to accompany the singers, who stand in the middle of the group. The songs span all those mentioned above, with *moppies* proving very popular.

Nagtroep *(minstrels) with parasols*

Malay Choirs

By the early part of the 20th century, a number of these choirs existed, carrying creative names such as Red Roses, Young Stars, Young Lions, Carnations and the All Blacks. These Malay choirs continued rather informally until 1939. In this year, members of various choirs met at 77 Wale Street, proposing a choral competition for the following year, to be hosted in the City Hall. The event saw eight choirs competing and it was a great success.

With the assistance of a Dr ID du Plessis (who had studied and written much on the Bo-Kaap although some within the Muslim community found his views somewhat patronising) and Benny Osler, a well-known Springbok rugby player of the time, an official body – the Malay Choirs Board – came into being. Benny Osler worked for the United Tobacco Company, and it was their initial sponsorship that enabled the board to preserve this choral tradition.

Today the Malay choirs attract a wide range of participants, varying in age from early twenties to, among the oldest members, late seventies or eighties. Choir members are usually all male; however, on New Year's Eve, when around 50 Malay choirs take to the streets as the *nagtroepe*, many women are keen to join in the fun. At the stroke of midnight they start their road march in District Six. Their route takes them past the Grand Parade to Adderley Street, up Wale Street and on to Rose Street in the Bo-Kaap. The procession turns around and eventually disperses in Plein Street about six hours later.

During the rest of the year the Malay choirs (also called *sangkore*) meet frequently to compose new songs and rehearse for the big event. The highlight of the year is the annual competition, which usually takes place in late January or February (unless *Ramadan* falls during that month). At this time the standard Malay choir is composed of about 60 members, including officials and the choir coach, who is responsible for the musical arrangements and has the final say in the choir's repertoire.

SINGING COMPETITIONS

There are four main categories in the competition itself: *moppies*, *Nederlandseliedjies*, junior solo and senior solo. During the competition the choirs are generally dressed in blazer and trousers, with a tie or bow tie, topped off with a white or red fez. Dress code is very important, and judges award marks for the best turned-out choir. Tying in with the dress code is a perpetual floating trophy – a silver fez donated in 1942 by Dr Du Plessis – for which the choirs compete every year. Through preliminary rounds and sectional finals, the choirs progress to the Grand Final, often held in the Good Hope Centre. Throughout, they sing without the aid of a conductor. And ironically, in the singing of the *Nederlandseliedjies*, the *ghoema* is not permitted as an accompaniment. In the *moppies* section, many classical pieces of music from composers such as Strauss or Brahms are taken and adapted, using comic lyrics in Afrikaans. Alternatively, the lyrics of present-day popular music are adapted – one famous *moppie* used the music to Roy Orbison's *Only the Lonely*. Taliep Petersen recalls that his initial fascination with, and talent for, music and singing developed through just such competitions.

Today there are probably in excess of 100 informal choirs and troupes around the Cape Peninsula. Currently 40 choirs are involved with the Cape Malay Board, making it the biggest multinational-multicultural organisation of its kind. Membership of the board is open to any individual, irrespective of his or her religious beliefs; currently about 70 per cent are of the Muslim faith and 30 per cent of other denominations.

Malay choirs linked to the Bo-Kaap include the Goodhopes, the Starlites, the Swans and the Young Stars. A demonstration choir, which is composed of members selected from the various affiliated choirs, has been widely acclaimed throughout South Africa and also internationally. The only year there was no official competition was 1979. Political unrest had reached such a point in South Africa the board reasoned: 'How can we keep on singing when people are being killed?'

A Christmas choir in the Bo-Kaap

Christmas Choirs

These choirs are a variation on the night minstrels. Similarly, they walk through the streets singing, but generally play hymns, marches and traditional carols. It gives some indication of just how integrated cultures have become – predominantly Muslim members celebrating Christian festivals and the New Year, as long as they don't coincide with the Muslim calendar. The first official organisation of the Christmas choirs, the City and Suburban Christmas Band Union, was formed in 1943.

Singers and musicians will often belong to the *nagtroepe*, a Christmas choir, an official Malay choir and a Coon troupe. Coaches who work with the choirs often teach the Coons building up to carnival time. It can be quite a costly business, though, with the Malay choir and Coons needing a different outfit each year.

MUSIC RUNS IN THE FAMILY

Salie Allie's family has long been associated with the musical tradition of the Bo-Kaap. In the 1940s and 1950s, Salie was a well-known composer of songs, including many *moppies* and *ghoemaliedjies*. He also coached Malay choirs and Coon troupes. His musical talent was passed on to his children who formed The Allie Brothers Continental Band, a popular acoustic guitar band with singers. The famous Greek singer, Nana Mouskouri, heard them on one occasion and asked two of the brothers, Yusuf and Armien, to accompany her to Europe to play with her backing band. Yusuf won an Oppenheimer scholarship to study at the Royal Academy of Music in London. Ultimately he became a full-time band member and travelled the world with Nana Mouskouri. Armien still lives in the Bo-Kaap, and remains as passionate about music as ever. He is a master on the guitar and other string instruments – his music makes angels dance!

Armien Allie, a master of classical guitar

THE NEW MOPPIES

One example of the new *moppies* (as detailed by Denis-Constant Martin in his paper, 'South Africa: Social history through the Moppies – Calling for research') sung by the *nagtroepe* is the very popular *Ons Hoor* – 'We can hear them'. It's a good example of a song with political overtones and a social conscience. When it was first performed on New Year's Eve, 1994, it looked towards the new era in South Africa and the end of apartheid. Through laughter, the song helped the community to come to terms with the major upheavals that were happening in the country. The last verses were added to the original version by the band, The Tulips, and pay tribute to the then future president of South Africa, Nelson Mandela (Madiba).

Ons Hoor – **We Can Hear Them**
Here they come, and all of them are doing the toyi toyi
We hear them, we hear them, we hear them, they are doing the toyi toyi
There's unrest in Nyanga, Khayelitsha and Langa
All over South Africa, they're doing the toyi toyi
We read in the newspapers
Cape Town is on fire
We see on TV
The squatter camps are burning
The riot squad was there
To chase them away
Oh la la la, oh la la la la

Before, we did not worry because everything was tax-free
Then came the GST and now it's the VAT
VAT on coffee, VAT on tea
There's VAT on meat and rice
But there's no VAT on reefers, no

The people stayed away from work for two days
COSATU said they will get their full salaries
One is walking in front with the flag in his hand
The others are behind
In the street, on to the Parade, they're all doing the toyi toyi
Come on people, let's toyi toyi *all together*
Viva Madiba, viva Madiba, viva Madiba, viva South Africa
We all want to say we love you,
Madiba.

Lyrics and song composed by Adam Samodien and Rashaad Maliek
English translation by Anwar Gambeno, musical director of The Tulips

Carnival time!

ape Town is the place to be at New Year … Besides the fun and festivities of the night minstrels, the main celebration anyone visiting Cape Town should not miss is the Coon Carnival. It takes place on 2 January (*Tweede Nuwe Jaar*) and may be compared to Mardi Gras in New Orleans and Rio, or the Nottinghill Carnival in London. The story goes that *Tweede Nuwe Jaar* was the day on which the Malay slaves were given time off because their masters celebrated on New Year's Day.

The slaves at the Cape were officially emancipated on 1 December 1834, followed by a four-year compulsory labour apprenticeship to their former slave masters until 1 December 1838.

The current form of the Coon Carnival (*Kaapse Klopse* in Afrikaans) dates back to the arrival of the American Confederacy ship, CSS *Alabama* in Cape Town in 1862. In America during the Civil War, groups of white entertainers were impersonating African-American slave minstrels. They blackened their faces with burnt corks and painted white around their eyes and lips to exaggerate those features; they also wore outfits in vibrant colours. These minstrels went by the name Coons. Although the term became racially derogatory, it is believed to have been borrowed from the North American racoon, a creature with white mask-like discs around the eyes. The name stuck. On board the CSS *Alabama* were a number of African-American slaves who entertained crowds at the docks in a similar fashion to the Coon troupes, and this revelry had a major impact on the former slaves at the Cape.

Later that year, in August 1862, the first organised stage show, 'Christy's Minstrels', took place at the Theatre Royal in Harrington Street. Minstrel shows became a forum for cultural exchange between black and white, American and European, African and American-European cultures. For similar reasons, such events became popular in South Africa. In his book *Coon Carnival, New Year in Cape Town, Past and Present* (David Philip), Denis-Constant Martin says: 'Superficially, it reinforced racial stereotypes and offered whites a medium of scorn and contempt for blacks. But deeper down, minstrelsy was in fact anti-authoritarian, imbued with youth and working-class rebellion.'

THE COONS COME TO THE CAPE

By 1887, around the time when Rasdien Cornelis and Sulaiman were collecting and recording songs, the first Cape Coon Carnival troupe was organised. With much applause from onlookers, a group of minstrels dressed in black-and-white satin costumes marched through the streets of Cape Town, singing as they went. With time it became

Voorlopers at the 2006 Carnival

typical for troupes, or *klopse*, to wear uniforms made out of bright synthetic material to emulate the first satin outfits. Some wear Panama hats or boaters and many also parade twirling parasols to match their colourful apparel.

A number of troupes have been associated with the Bo-Kaap. In 1989 the Goodhope Entertainers troupe was started in Van der Meulen Street. From early July onwards they would start practising, meeting every Wednesday and Sunday. Typically, there were 600–700 people taking part in the festivities leading up to the Coon Carnival.

Each year, on 2 January, the procession usually starts around 10:00 in Darling Street marching past the Grand Parade as thousands of onlookers throng the streets, revelling in the party atmosphere. The troupes are later ferried by bus to Green Point Stadium where they compete for the Carnival's Best Troupe awards.

Voorlopers (literally, forewalkers) lead each troupe, throwing their batons in the air and doing intricate dance routines, keeping the crowds enthralled. Often a child or young person dressed in a similar outfit to the *voorloper* mimics his steps, in this way learning the tricks of the trade. Many troupes also have a *moffie* (Cape slang for a gay male) dressed in women's clothing, following the *voorloper*. He acts as a mascot for the minstrels, bringing them good luck.

Every year, each troupe adopts a new colour scheme. People in the community are kept busy stitching the outfits right up until the big celebration on *Tweede Nuwe Jaar*. The most recent new troupe was the Santam District Six, formed in 2005. Although the name suggests otherwise, most people in the troupe came from the Bo-Kaap. In the 2006 Carnival competition, they were voted first out of 15 troupes in section two; overall, they achieved third place in the competition.

MADIBA LENDS HIS MAGIC

For a period, many of the intellectual elite of the Cape coloured community boycotted the carnival. Today, some still view it as inferior to the Malay Choirs, but after Nelson Mandela became patron of the event, the Carnival was given a new sense of social acceptance.

The event has grown considerably over the years, so much so that by 2006 there were up to 13 000 participants in the New Year celebrations. The majority of the troupes (169 of them) are represented by the Kaapse Karnavaal Assosiasie (Cape Carnival Association). In addition, two breakaway organisations, the Kaapse Klopse Karnavaal Association and the Mitchells Plain Youth Development Minstrel Board, represent a much smaller number of troupes. Although Capetonians still call it the Coon Carnival, local authorities prefer to call the festival the Cape Town Minstrel Carnival as some find the term 'coon' offensive.

Trumpet player with the District Six Entertainers

Islamic calligraphy
Development of the written word

It is not just in song but also in the written word that culture within the Bo-Kaap has found a defining means of expression. Unlike many other religions that have used figurative images to portray their basic beliefs, there is a highly developed use of calligraphy within Islam, principally Arabic script. According to contemporary studies, Arabic belongs to the Semitic alphabetical scripts in which mainly the consonants are represented. It evolved in a comparatively brief time span and today the use of the Arabic alphabet is second only to the Roman alphabet.

The Nabateans were seminomadic Arabs who dwelt in an area extending from Sinai and North Arabia to southern Syria. Their empire included the major cities of Hijr, Petra and Busra. Although the Nabatean empire ended in 105CE, its language and writing had a profound impact on the early development of Arabic scripts. Archaeologists and linguists have analysed Nabatean inscriptions that represent an advanced transitional stage which led to the development of Arabic scripts such as the Um al-Jimal, dating from about 250CE, and the Namarah of famous pre-Islamic poet Imru' al-Qays, dating from 328CE. Other inscriptions from Um al-Jimal, from the 6th century onwards, confirm the derivation of the Arabic script from the Nabatean, and point to the birth of distinctive Arabic writing forms. North Arabic script was first introduced and established in the northeastern part of Arabia. During the 5th century, Arabian nomadic tribes living in the areas of Hirah and Anbar used this script extensively. By the early part of the 6th century, North Arabic script had reached Hijaz in western Arabia. Bishr Ibn Abd al-Malik and his father-in-law, Harb Ibn Umayyah, are credited with introducing and popularising the use of this script among the Prophet Muhammad's tribe, Quraysh.

As the teachings of Islam spread beyond the boundaries of the Arabian Peninsula, an enormous number of people worldwide became Muslim. These new converts interpreted the art of writing according to their own cultural and aesthetic systems – it became an abstract expression of Islam. The shapes and sizes of the script became a thing of beauty, as scholar Yasin Hamid Safadi (1978) explains:

The primacy of the word in Islam is reflected in the virtually universal application of calligraphy. Writing is given pride of place on all kinds of objects – objects of everyday use as well as entire wall surfaces, mosque furniture, the interiors and exteriors of mosques, tombs, and al-Ka'bah, *the most famous sanctuary of Islam.*

Arabic lettering has now achieved a high level of sophistication, and Arabic scripts can vary from flowing cursive styles like Naskh and Thuluth to the angular Kufi. Within the Bo-Kaap a number of different writing styles appear on the walls, windows and minarets of mosques and religious buildings. Most of the inscriptions are not only from the Qur'an but also the Hadith. Calligraphic artwork is also a prominent feature in many homes; the ornately inscribed texts form eye-catching focal points and are an omnipresent reminder of cultural heritage.

The entire Qur'an in Arabic script

'God is great'
Achmat Soni, painted relief

LOCAL TALENT

The boundaries of Islamic calligraphy are not clearly defined but are, rather, a dynamic evolving art form. In South Africa, the members of one family have established themselves as calligraphic painters par excellence. In 1982, Achmat Soni, inspired by his reading of the Qur'an, created his first piece of calligraphic art based on the opening chapter, the *Al-Fatiha*. From this, the distinctive Soni Art studio developed, its initial direction influenced by the cultural isolation of the apartheid years. Achmat acknowledges that it was partly due to this sense of isolation that he was able to adopt a style so unique and different.

Since its inception, Soni Art has expanded to include Achmat, Shaheen Soni and Tasneem Chilwan-Soni, each contributing their own personal touch. Achmat's style has evolved through his awareness of differences and by absorbing the best in both Eastern and Western styles in his own calligraphic style and execution. Much of his more recent work also shows the influence of the great modern calligraphers of Indonesia and Malaysia. Variety and a need to recreate are clearly observed too in Achmat's Ndebele-influenced calligraphy, which gives Islamic art an African dimension that has not been seen before. As an experimentalist, he uses layered texture to bring his calligraphy to life.

Soni artworks are popular in many Bo-Kaap homes and extensive calligraphy exhibitions have been held both here and abroad, including Pakistan, Tunisia, Syria, Saudi Arabia and Malaysia. Works by Achmat and his family have also been commissioned for many South African mosques, including the Bo-Kaap's Hanafee (1990) and Nurul Islam (2003) mosques. The studios of Soni Art are now based at 3 Soni Road, Crawford, Athlone (tel: 021 697 3941) where a wide range of Islamic calligraphic art may be viewed and purchased.

Achmat Soni at work

Art and Political Transformation

Major political unrest prevailed in South Africa during the late 1970s, which brought about widespread violence. At the time, Ishmael Achmat, a spray painter and panel beater by trade, lived in the Bo-Kaap. As secretary to the Schotsche Kloof Civic Association, Ishmael wondered how he could play his part in helping to restore order. On 29 May 1979, he decided that the only practical thing he could do was to write to then state president, PW Botha.

This letter insisted that the president dismantle apartheid, and that his approach become a virtuous one in order for peace to prevail in South Africa. Ishmael considered it worth the try. When he received official acknowledgement of his correspondence, it spurred him on to write to the president again. This time he requested a colour photograph so that he could do a portrait of the president!

Not having painted a portrait before, Ishmael had no idea what he was letting himself in for – he figured that with God's help, he was up to the challenge, though. Several weeks later another letter from De Tuynhuys, the president's official state office, included a black-and-white photograph. Not quite what he'd hoped for … but he decided to go ahead with the portrait, using it somehow to make his statement to the president. The photograph's dual tones prompted him to do his painting in three colours: black, white and brown. In his mind the symbolism represented the fact that black and white are separate forms, and if combined do not make brown. This portrait completed, he wrote again to the president, telling him he'd painted him the colour of rock to show steadfastness. In 1980 he met with PW Botha in the then Hendrick Verwoerd Building and presented him with the painting, to much admiration from the president. As a token of his thanks, he presented Ishmael with a pen, which in turn proved to be highly symbolic – thus began a correspondence, which lasted for many years, between the man viewed as the epitome of apartheid and an ordinary citizen of colour fighting for change.

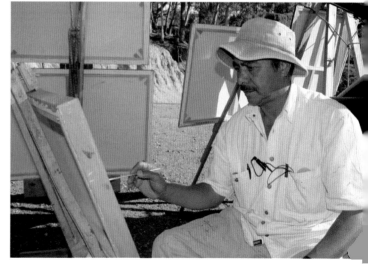

Ishmael Achmat at work on the slopes of Table Mountain

The original signed photograph of PW alongside Ishmael's portrait

POLITICAL MESSAGES VIA ART

Ishmael decided next to do a painting of Table Mountain to express the potential freedom of the country. As he painted, he wrote a 53-page manuscript to the president in which he discussed the historical composition of the people of South Africa, and the humanitarian aspects of how one should relate to one's fellow man, irrespective of creed or colour. The first time he submitted this manuscript, it was intercepted by state officials who sent him a terse reply. Undaunted, Ishmael tried a different approach. He befriended PW Botha's sister-in-law, Mrs Rousseau, and later persuaded her to give a copy personally to the president.

By March 1985, violence in South Africa had escalated to such an extent that the government was forced to augment a stretched police force with the army. On 20 July 1985, President Botha announced that a State of Emergency would be imposed on 36 magisterial districts starting at midnight. It was the first time since the 1960 Sharpeville crisis that the government had had to resort to such extreme measures. In Durban, the murder of a civil rights lawyer led to angry confrontations between the United Democratic Front and the Inkatha Freedom

Party. Within four days, 50 people were dead and hundreds of buildings had been burnt. The trouble spread to Cape Town (and the Bo-Kaap), where more than 30 people died in African and coloured areas.

In order to stem the violence, the government closed nearly half the coloured schools and colleges in the Western Cape. Between September 1984 and January 1986, more than 950 people had been killed as a direct result of political unrest.

Throughout this period, Ishmael kept up his correspondence with the state president. In his last letter, dated 29 January 1987, Ishmael wrote:

> *I appeal to you to accept the fact that there is no white man, there has not been and never shall be. The term 'white man' belongs to the colonialists of the past and it is important, Mr Botha, that you should rid yourself of these stigmas. In reality South Africa consists of many different traditions.*

On 18 January 1989, President Botha suffered a stroke, which precipitated him into resigning from his position as state president. FW de Klerk became the new president and leader of the National Party. As the wave of change swept through the country, Nelson Mandela was released from prison and the regime of apartheid was finally laid to rest.

Ishmael Achmat has gone on to do portraits of presidents Mandela and Thabo Mbeki. He firmly believes that art should be used as a form of positive change. In his words, 'A lot of people throughout my community hated Botha, but I felt that hate on hate could not change people, but love on hate, or forgiveness on hate, can.'

After an article appeared in the *Cape Argus* in May 2004 about Ishmael's special association with the former president, PW Botha rang Ishmael and thanked him for his letters over the eight-year period and for the inspiration they had provided.

Despite the fact that he has never had any formal art training, in 2003 Ishmael took up painting full-time. He can frequently be seen with his canvases near the lower cable station on the slopes of Table Mountain.

Ishmael Achmat presenting his portraiture to Nelson Mandela

Ishmael's portrait of President Mbeki

107

Reflections on a Rich Cultural Heritage

ം൭ᴑᴑ൭ᴑ

The Melting Pot of Nations

ം൭ᴑᴑ൭ᴑ

The melting pot of nations
Of cultures far and wide
Of merging minds and values
To a new era abide

The restless soul forever searching
For new adventures in its realm
The energies of life forever connecting
Like the melodies of Orphean

The ethos of nations so varied and rich
Grows richer when cultures are shared
To appreciate the importance of other traditions
Without our own values impaired

Abdeya da Costa

The making of a people

uring the 18th and early 19th centuries, over 60 000 slaves were brought to the Cape. From the table on page 21, it can be seen that the majority of these slaves originated in Africa, India and the East Indies, with less than 1 per cent coming from Malaya, or present-day Malaysia. Traditional languages of the people from the Indian Ocean basin included Melayu and Malayo-Portuguese. Thus, it was identification with the commonality of language rather than the origin of these slaves that gave birth to the collective term, Malay. The first recorded written use of the classification, Malay, was in the census of the Cape in 1875.

BIRTH OF A LANGUAGE

Language played an interesting transformative role. Although many languages and dialects from the various regions of origin were spoken, Melayu had become the common language amongst the slaves. However, when communicating with their masters, the slaves were required to speak Dutch. According to Achmat Davids, this meant that the language was a merging of mixed ancestries – Dutch and Melayu with the spoken Afrikaans of the Cape Muslim community. By the time of the Bo-Kaap's embryonic beginnings, Afrikaans had replaced Melayu as the spoken language of the slaves. Melayu was still used predominantly for Muslim writing and teaching, but by 1815, in most of the *madrassahs* (Muslim schools) Afrikaans had replaced Melayu. This transformation was almost complete by 1830, when the journalist CE Boniface described Afrikaans as the language of the 'non-whites'. The term 'Malay' denoting the people themselves persisted, however, even though many found it derogatory.

THE HERITAGE OF SKILLED CRAFTSMANSHIP

It was not language alone that these immigrants brought with them. Many were skilled craftsmen, which the Dutch exploited for their own benefit. Fine examples of carving – the product of the expert workmanship of these slaves – exist in many Cape Dutch manor homes. The best Malaysian wood-carvers came from Terengganu and Kelantan, where this artistry was passed down through generations. The craft comprises fine carving (*ukiran halus*), such as that found on many Cape Dutch bed-heads and the top of cupboards, and rough carving (*ukiran kasar*) featured on larger pieces of furniture, on ornate ceremonial coaches and in house construction.

Fine carving was completed in four stages. The design was first traced out, and then the outline chiselled into the wood. Next, unwanted parts were cut out and finally the piece would be sculpted into an exquisitely beautiful work of art. In the Bo-Kaap, this tradition was handed down within families although there are now very few who still practise. Craftsman Armien Allie is one of the last great wood-carvers living there today. His furniture displays carvings of exotic birds, fish, dolphins and creeping grapevine. Intricate details pay testament to the work of an artist.

Many slaves, free blacks and those emancipated from slavery were employed in construction, although they probably had little influence in respect of architectural styles. The first houses in the area to have a strong Cape Dutch influence were those built under the direction of Jan de Waal, in the 1760s. At that time, this residential area was called Walendorp and the homes belonged to white artisans. The Bo-Kaap Museum (see page 6) in Wale Street belongs to this original group of houses, dating back as it does to 1768. Plans of Cape Town drawn up in 1791 already indicate how the area was starting to expand, and soon this expansion acquired the name Upper Cape, or Bo-Kaap.

THE UNIFYING FORCE OF FAITH

Muslim slaves used to secretly worship in private houses and at the quarry in Chiappini Street. When they were at last permitted to practise their religion openly, the community began to regroup. In 1798, Auwal Mosque was built in Dorp Street and acted as a focal point, functioning as the centre of sociocultural activities. Mosques had always been central to the Muslim community, and now, at last, they had their own. More so than anything else, the introduction of Auwal and subsequent mosques was responsible for this area turning rapidly into a predominantly Muslim community – and the Bo-Kaap began to take on an Eastern flavour.

In the early 1800s, when the Tana Baru land was given to the community as a burial ground, traditional Muslim funerals became a common sight here in the Bo-Kaap. According to Muslim practice at that time, the body of the deceased was given an ablution ceremony, *abdas*, followed by a ritual cleansing, *ghusl*. The body was then wrapped, and after prayers placed on a bier and carried shoulder high to the Tana Baru.

Mourners waiting for the funeral bier to pass
(Reproduced from the National Archive, E9048)

111

IDENTITY THROUGH
CULTURAL DRESS

Traditional everyday dress for many members of the Muslim community included *kaparang* shoes and a *toding* conical hat for the men. *Kaparang* were wooden-soled, open-toed sandals originally worn by Muslims in their native lands in the East Indies before being taken captive. Examples of these shoes may be seen in the Bo-Kaap Museum. In 1861, the fez was introduced to the Cape by Turkish missionaries, and it eventually replaced the *toding*. From that time on, fezzes were manufactured at the Cape for over a century. In later years, the Jassiem family was especially well known for its fez-making – but sadly all that remains of this art is the beautiful heavy brass equipment once used to make the fezzes. Examples of the *kaparang*, the *toding* and the brass equipment used to make the fez may be seen at the Bo-Kaap Museum.

The fez became a traditional part of male dress
(Reproduced from the National Archive, E8693)

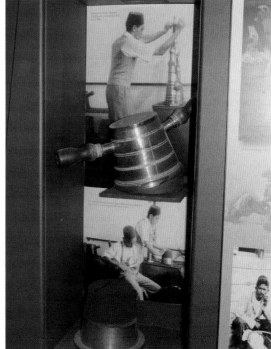

Fez-making display at the Bo-Kaap Museum

Early photograph of a horse-drawn carriage in the Bo-Kaap

THE MALAY QUARTER DEVELOPS A PERSONALITY

With the abolition of slavery in 1834, many ex-slaves moved into the Bo-Kaap and the community rapidly expanded. The cobbled streets resounded with the clop-clop of horses' hooves; the horses were stabled in Rose Street where they served the local community, and were also used for ceremonial functions. By the mid-19th century, rows of houses with attached courtyards were well established. The area came to be known as the Malay Quarter – defined to the west and east by Dorp and Strand streets respectively, and stretching roughly north from Buitengracht Street up the slopes to include Chiappini Street. Most houses were dated between 1760 and 1850. The people living here were employed in a variety of trades, from building and carpentry to shoemaking, tailoring and fishing.

By the end of the 19th century, South Africa was a flourishing country. The prospect of a new life attracted many people from India and the East Indies to venture across the seas and set up their own businesses here. One such person was Jaga Jivan Parmar, a cobbler from Gujarat State in India. Together with a group of about 25–30 men, he left India in 1902 on board a ship to seek his fortune on the distant shores of Africa. Arriving at Maputo in Mozambique, the group made the long journey by train and on foot to Durban. Many stayed there, assimilating into the Indian community, but Jivan continued on to Cape Town where he joined a small Hindu community. He set up his business in the Bo-Kaap, and it became the thriving Rocksole Shoe sales and repairs business. Today Jivan's grandchildren and great-grandchildren run Rocksole.

AFTER DETERIORATION COMES REGENERATION

As more and more people moved into the Bo-Kaap, the quality of the houses started to deteriorate. In 1934 almost the entire Malay Quarter was proclaimed a slum in terms of the Slums Act. The main reason behind this was the need of the city to expand – and the Malay Quarter provided the perfect space. Development began further up the hill, the intention being to move families out of the Malay Quarter so that it could be levelled. The building projects of Schotsche Kloof, Stadzicht and Schoone Kloof were amalgamated with the Bo-Kaap – although today the demarcation is not exactly clear.

Heiliger Lane, off Church Street, 1950s
(P. Lyons, Reproduced from the National Archive)

Schotsche Kloof The Dutch East India Company farm was on a terrace above the Malay Quarter. Between 1938 and 1942, 198 subeconomic flats were built to house the Muslim community. A special feature of the flats were the additional rooms that provided for the ritual cleaning of the dead, called *toekamandi kamers*. The term *toekamandi* is Indonesian in origin, meaning 'person who washes the dead'; *kamer* is Dutch for 'room'. A primary school and community centre were also built to service the needs of the people.

Stadzicht This zone, at the top end of Longmarket Street, adjacent to the Schotsche Kloof flats, was also once farmland owned by the VOC. In the 1940s, it developed into a small home-ownership area.

Schoone Kloof The houses here were built mainly from the 1920s onwards, although a few are much older. This is the western region of Bo-Kaap, and today it is almost entirely privately owned. The area includes St Monica's, originally a maternity hospital but today functioning as an old age home. Also in Schoone Kloof are the St Paul's Anglican Primary School and Nurul Huda mosque, constructed in 1958.

Historian Dr ID du Plessis, who did much to chronicle the life of the Bo-Kaap, was involved in raising funds to help restore a number of houses in the Malay Quarter. Despite their intended fate for demolition, in 1962 the entire area was given a lucky reprieve when it was declared a national monument.

THE GROUP AREAS ACT

In 1950, the National Party, who formed the South African government, passed the Group Areas Act. It was this move, together with the creation of the homelands, that firmly established the inhumane policy of apartheid, setting the tone for racial segregation throughout the country. The Act applied to members of all racial groups and provided for the imposition of control over ownership and occupation of land and buildings within South Africa. It established a Group Areas Board to advise the Minister of Planning on the demarcation of Group Areas for members of the various racial groups.

This meant that all white, black, coloured and Asian people in South Africa would have to live in zones allocated to members of their population group. Ownership of property and business rights would be confined to those areas. The Bo-Kaap was designated a Malay area, so all non-Malays had to move out. A possible reason for the Malay designation was that many expert tailors lived here – highly convenient for Parliament and the Law Courts, which required the manufacture of official robes. The stables in Rose Street, too, provided horses for state horse-drawn carriages. The last horses to be stabled here were done so in the mid-1950s.

Although hotly contested within the Muslim community, in some ways the Group Areas Act may be seen to have done the people of the Bo-Kaap a favour. The area was rapidly deteriorating and the City Council was quite happy to demolish it in order to allow for expansion of the CBD. Ironically, when the Act came into force, most of the Malay community living there were effectively protected from eviction. The classification of people according to colour and race was very inexact, however. Some Indian members of the community applied to the board and were reclassified as Malay.

The Group Areas Board also wielded control over social gatherings – for example, anyone in the community wishing to hold a wedding had first to make application to the board and submit a full guest list. If approved, inspectors were sent out to make sure the list was adhered to, and also that it did not become a political gathering.

From the time the Act was introduced, the face of the Bo-Kaap changed. Shops closed down and others took their place. In the 1960s and 1970s many of the houses in various states of disrepair were torn down, and the City Council was obliged by the provincial government to restore the area. It was around this time that the brightly coloured edifices of many of the houses started to appear in the Bo-Kaap.

The restoration proved to be a blessing for the people who were not able to afford upkeep and maintenance of their houses. By the 1980s, many people living in the area were finally able to buy their own houses, newly restored. When the African National Congress came to power in 1994, the Group Areas Act was repealed.

Shortmarket Street, 1950s
(P. Lyons, Reproduced from the National Archive)

Bo-Kaap
A generational legacy

uan Guru (Imam Abdullah *Kadi* Abdus Salaam) was one of the most influential early Sunni Muslim settlers at the Cape. A prince and descendant of the Sultan of Morocco, he arrived in 1780 as a political captive of the Dutch, and was immediately incarcerated on Robben Island. There he expounded his philosophy, in his writings entitled *Ma'rifah al-Islam wa Al Iman*. Over 600 pages in length, it explores, amongst other issues, principles of Islamic law, the will of God, and examines a social system where slaves and their free black slave-owners could live together harmoniously. He also made several copies of the Holy Qur'an from memory. On his release from Robben Island, he settled in Dorp Street in the Bo-Kaap. There was a profound need amongst the Muslim slaves for a school, or *madrassah*, to teach them on religious and cultural issues. In 1793, with a handful of

The Holy Qur'an written by Tuan Guru and kept in Auwal Mosque

students, Tuan Guru set up the first such school in South Africa from his home in Dorp Street. His *Ma'rifah* became the school's main textbook; by 1842, Islam accounted for one-third of the population's religious beliefs.

Abdeya da Costa, from her beautiful house in Dorp Street close to the Auwal Mosque where she was born and has lived all her life, can trace her ancestry back to Tuan Guru. She is a direct fourth-generation descendant of the illustrious scholar – so who better to give us an insight into what life was like growing up and living in the Bo-Kaap?

STORY OF A BO-KAAP HOME

Abdeya was raised in a family of nine children, three of whom unfortunately died in early infancy. Her house, typical of many townhouses in the Bo-Kaap built in the 18th and 19th centuries and representing the Dutch architecture of the time, has a high *stoep* in front, with steps that lead up from the road. Originally, it was a single-storey building. Her front door opens onto a long passageway running the length of the house with rooms leading off this. At the back of the house, the kitchen connects with an enclosed courtyard, flanked on either side by walls separating it from neighbouring courtyards. Abdeya recalls that in many of the houses that had large courtyards, the women would provide a laundering service, taking in washing from nearby white families. Although there were specific washhouses in the area, it served as an additional income for many families.

As a young child, Abdeya remembers the house always being a bustle of activity. 'My father was a sheikh and ran a *madrassah* in our house. We had benches on either side of the passageway; many people would come and go. In the mornings, young preschool children arrived to learn the Arabic alphabet and very basic principles of the Islamic faith. They did this often through simple songs and stories. Later in the day, older children and teenagers would come from school to learn how to read the Qur'an and prepare for the *tamat* ceremony. Evening classes for the adults would include lessons on the principles of Islamic etiquette and such concepts as *taqwah*, or piety, and how to attain it through fearing God and being submissive to his commands.'

Abdeya's father

A HAPPY CHILDHOOD

Childhood images that remain in her head bring back the powerful community spirit that always prevailed. 'What I remember most about the Bo-Kaap from my childhood is the sense of community and the willingness of everyone to collectively help each other. Dorp Street was full of life – *Motjie* [an affectionate term for an older woman] Jockera

Abdeya's mother and sister

lived opposite us. She used to set up a stall in her yard to sell fruit and vegetables. People would collect there to hear all the latest news and gossip. She kept us all informed. In other houses further up the street lived tailors and dressmakers. The Keraan family were well known for their tailoring skills – but there were many gifted people in the community. Most of the work they did was for white people living in Cape Town; however, they also made exquisite wedding dresses for the people living in the Bo-Kaap. My sister also used to make dresses and eventually went to Saudi Arabia to make dresses for the royal family there. I would go to collect fabric for her from the mainly Jewish-owned shops in Hanover Street in District Six. I loved to look at the fabrics and the dresses, and imagine what it would be like to have a shop of my own where I could sell them. But in the days of apartheid, this seemed like a far-off dream.

'My mother was an entrepreneur and knew how to make money to support her family in a wide range of ways. She used to make *tameletjies* and *koeksisters* and sell these in the neighbourhood, or get us children to sell them to our friends at school. I remember that she would buy perfumes from stores in Cape Town and sell them to women locally. During apartheid we could not use any of the "white" beaches, so she would hire buses and collect people in the neighbourhood to go on day trips to places like Macassar beach.'

When Abdeya's father became *imam* at the Palm Tree Mosque in 1937, he immersed himself in the duties that went with that role. 'Just after a child was born in the community, the *imams* would be brought for the *doepmaal*, or naming ceremony. The parents would place the child on a tray surrounded by flowers and carry him to my father, who would take the baby in his arms and make a sign of peace on his forehead. Then he would recite the *shahada* [or affirmation of Islam] in the child's ear.'

ENTERING INTO ADULTHOOD

The *tamat* ceremony was very important to every young person in the community. 'We were required to learn Arabic in order that we could read the Qur'an in its original form. This meant that our grammar, pronunciation and intonation had to be perfect. I was 13 at the time of my *tamat* ceremony. On the day, I wore a long white dress with a Medora headdress that had come from Mecca. I remember that there was great excitement in the neighbourhood. I arrived at the mosque in a carriage led by white horses. The boys who were doing the ceremony wore typical Arabic clothes and a *sorbaan* – which is a turban normally worn by the *hadji* (or pilgrim) coming from Mecca. There were two attendants with us. One carried the Qur'an in a special cover; the other held a satin cushion with elaborate embroidery upon which the Qur'an was placed for us to read. A number of *imams* and judges were in the mosque to examine us. We were each given a chapter of the Qur'an to read, and afterwards we were asked questions. Once we had passed, we returned to the waiting carriage to be driven through the streets with bells ringing, and our friends and neighbours came out to great us. There was a real atmosphere of celebration.'

Abdeya's brother and two attendants dressed for tamat

THE CHANGING FACE OF THE NEIGHBOURHOOD

Abdeya recollects the changes that took place in the area as the city expanded and the government attempted to declare it a slum zone. 'Before the Slums Act of 1934, the Bo-Kaap had a different look and feel. There was a mansion occupied by a German family, and the English upper class also lived here. The Muslim people living in the area were dignified. There was a hidden agenda for the central government wanting to turn the Quarter into a slum. They wanted to move the Muslims out of the Bo-Kaap because this was a strategic location in the heart of the city, and then sell these houses at a cheap price to the poorer white government workers. A large part of the area was condemned for so-called 'health reasons', and the owners of the properties were forced to vacate their premises and move to the Cape Flats or other so-called 'coloured' areas. Before further damage to the area, parties interested in maintaining the historical value of the area stepped in and the process stopped. The empty houses were left to decay and depreciate. Afterwards, people of undesirable status were moved in to occupy these houses at a minimal rental – and further rot set in, so that these did, in fact, become slum houses. This had the effect of making some of the Muslim community despondent and they moved of their own volition. Some plots were levelled and remain vacant to this day.'

(P. Lyons, Reproduced from the National Archive)

Wale Street in the 1950s

CELEBRATIONS OF MARRIAGE

Abdeya married in 1955. In the Bo-Kaap, activities leading up to a wedding were very different to Western preparations. 'Traditionally the groom's father had to approach the prospective father-in-law and interview him. If the father was deceased, then the eldest son would become the *wakiel*, meaning that he assumed the duties of the head of the household. When both parties were satisfied, an official announcement of the engagement, or *lambaar*, was made. Everything was very formal.'

Once the engagement was confirmed, the couple would visit all the family members to tell them that the wedding was going to take place, and each family would decide upon their gifts. Often dresses were given to the bride, which could not be refused and had to be worn on the day. The trousseau (which comprises nightgown, nightwear and underwear) was another very important part of the new bride's gifts. They were normally made of fine satin and elaborately embroidered. One week before the wedding, when the gifts had been delivered, a special celebration would happen at the bride's house called a *struikery*. At this, the trousseau is ironed and laid out on trestle tables to be viewed, along with the other gifts. In the evening 'trimmers' would come into the home and decorate it with colourful crepe paper. As they worked, they sang *bruidsliedjies*, or bridal songs.

'On the big day, the bridegroom attends the mosque in the morning, where he sits in front of the *imam* with male relatives, neighbours and friends around him. This is when the actual official ceremony takes place. The bride does not go to the mosque, but meets her guests at her parents' home. Once the ceremony at the mosque is complete, the groom arrives at the reception to greet his wife and the guests. During the day she will go to the houses of her relatives who have given dresses, where she

changes and returns to the reception in one of the new dresses. The reception will last most of the day and the bride normally changes her dress three or four times!'

Abdeya's fascination with dresses and fabrics continued during the course of her life. After working at Super Tex in Plein Street for a number of years, she was finally able to realise her dream of opening her own dress shop. In 1973, she opened her first boutique on Main Road, Claremont. More than 30 years and five shops later, having been inspired by the entrepreneurial spirit of her mother all those years ago, she is still in the fashion business.

Welfare in the Community
Sharifa's Story

To many people living within the Bo-Kaap, Sharifa Fredericks' name is synonymous with community care. She is driven by her seemingly boundless energy and innate sense of inspiration as she organises a number of schemes designed to improve the health or welfare of many sectors of the Bo-Kaap's population.

Sharifa runs an elderly day-care centre in the grounds of the Vista High School in Military Road, which caters for 25 members living within the Bo-Kaap, aged from 55 to 87 years. Now in its eighth year, it runs every Monday and Wednesday morning. Helpers at the centre have been trained at the Sports Science Institute based in Newlands, and do physical activities and a range of crafts with the members. In conjunction with Age in Action, Sharifa organises an annual sports day, which has groups come from other centres in Bellville, Kensington, Joe Slovo, De Noon, Salt River, Maitland and Brooklyn. 'This is a lot of fun for everyone involved, and sees quite a healthy level of competition – even amongst our older members!' Sharifa laughs.

She feels it also important for people to gain a sense of pride through the learning of new skills that benefit themselves as well as the wider community. With this in mind, the day-care centre teaches the principles and application of aromatherapy, which has turned out to be very popular with all the members.

'In the hectic pace of modern life, it is very easy for generations to become disconnected. We aim at this centre to try to bridge that gap,' says Sharifa. One approach has been her Adopt-a-Granny programme, which sees students at the high school meeting with the day-care members to record and compile their stories. This serves to reconnect different generations, since many of these children do not grow up with older family members in the home.

The breakdown of family structure has also resulted in other problems within the community. The level of drug abuse by young people in the Bo-Kaap has risen, unfortunately, spurred on by a lack of opportunities and recreational facilities. 'We need to actively educate our young people about the dangers they face by using drugs,' says Sharifa, who is a firm supporter of the Bo-Kaap Anti-drug Coordinating Committee, which offers free drug counselling.

NURTURING PHYSICAL AND MENTAL HEALTH

As far as Sharifa is concerned, health and welfare are inextricably entwined. In 1994 she was on the health committee set up for home-based care in the Bo-Kaap. She is also on the Civic Committee for Health Education, a state health-based organisation that gives talks on health. As chairperson of the health committee for the third year and as a board member of the Somerset Hospital in Green Point, Sharifa actively raises funds to supply essential equipment to the hospital. The Somerset Hospital is the primary 24-hour public healthcare centre for the people of the Bo-Kaap. The only clinic serving the Bo-Kaap is a satellite one at Schotsche Kloof Civic Centre, which is mainly for family planning and paediatric cases.

On Tuesdays, Sharifa is involved with hospice at the Somerset Hospital. Hospice was started in the Bo-Kaap in October 1996. Today it has an Aids centre at the hospital, which includes a child protection centre and a 24-hour district surgeon. A trauma/rape centre also operates from the hospital and Sharifa is involved with the Abused and Battered Women's Forum, which meets in private homes. The well-known old St Monica's Maternity Hospital is now a home for abused and battered elderly people from the Bo-Kaap and also outside of the area. It caters for over-sixties and offers long-term, live-in self-catering for 20–25 people.

Working with the community means actively going out into the community. On Thursdays Sharifa does home visits for Social Services referrals and the Alzheimer's Association. Monday afternoons see her at the Advice Office set up in one of the local mosques in September 2005, which aims to give practical social and legal advice. As an extension of this role, she works at the trauma unit of the South African Police Service for one week in the month, when two people are on duty to do trauma counselling.

During *Ramadan*, Sharifa runs a soup kitchen in the Civic Centre in Pentz Street. She hopes that this will link up with Social Services so that it can be run throughout the year. Other feeding initiatives are run by the Nurul Islam Mosque, which provides food parcels for the needy in the community with the *imam's* support, once a month. The families of children learning the Qur'an at the mosque in preparation for their *tamat* help to pay for these food parcels.

This spirit of care giving in the Bo-Kaap is admirable, and the primary drive behind health and welfare in the community is in large part due to Sharifa.

TB's Angel of Mercy

Tuberculosis (TB) is still a health issue for certain people living in the Bo-Kaap, particularly those who are squatting or living on very limited funds. Sharifa Fredericks has been an area treatment supporter for the TB DOTS programme (Direct, Observe, Treatment, Short Course) for the past two years. The symptoms of tuberculosis (a persistent cough) are often very similar to colds and flu. Patients are diagnosed with a sputum test at the clinic in Chapel Street, Woodstock, on Mondays and Wednesdays. Children under the age of six have a skin test done if they've been in contact with a TB-positive case.

The first time they are diagnosed, adults are placed on a six-month course, with two months of injections at Green Point Day Hospital. If they are confirmed positive again after the initial course, the second course extends for eight months. Once confirmed with tuberculosis, those people living in the Bo-Kaap go to Sharifa every morning from 07:00 until 09:00, when she ensures that they take the correct medication. Children diagnosed with TB come in the afternoon after school to take their medication. One week before adults finish their six-month course they are sent to be retested; further confirmation is achieved by means of X-rays.

The daring dance of the swords

Of all the traditions associated with the Bo-Kaap, *Ratiep* (alternatively called *Khalifa* or *Chalifah*) is probably the one most shrouded in mystery. Originally it was a religious ceremony performed in honour of Abdul Kadir Beker and it resembles the *barong* dance of Bali. The name has its derivation in the word *khalif* or *caliph*, a title given to the successors of Muhammad as rulers of Islam. As part of the ritual, the leader blesses the swords and other instruments used, praying while the dance is performed.

It is still occasionally celebrated in the Bo-Kaap, although many *imams* look unfavourably on the practice – perhaps for reasons made clear in the following account of a ceremony described in the *Illustrated London News* on 18 August 1888. Note that the reference to 'tom-tom' drums most probably describes the *ghoema*, and some words – notably *khalifa* – have a variation in spelling.

Performing the Ratiep 'Kalifa'

A large number of Malays, descendants of those brought from the Islands of the Dutch East Indies in former times when the Dutch ruled at the Cape of Good Hope, form part of the population of Cape Town.

On April 24, not only for the first time, these people of an Asiatic race, in the chief city of the British South African Colony, exhibited a public performance of their extraordinary revels and orgies, sword-dances, knife-dances, and tricks with a variety of dangerous weapons, called the 'Kalifa' and originally connected with a religious festival. It took place in the Exhibition Building at Cape Town, where the stage of the large hall had been fitted for the occasion.

Palm trees stood on either side of the proscenium and the stage was fitted with Mohammedan symbols and a miniature mosque-like structure, behind which were a number of Malay singers; while seated round the stage were the drummers, who with the tom-tom kept up a continual boom, from which the actors took their time. All the performers in the Kalifa were dressed in white, with green sashes across the chest. The whole representation was under the charge of Hadji Saydien, who also prescribed at the celebration twenty-five years ago.

The proceedings opened with exhibitions of agility with knives. The Malays, about twelve in number, ranged themselves in two rows on the stage, facing each other. In each hand was a dagger, and, at a given signal, the tom-toms beat, the choir sang a monotonous lay, and the acrobats commenced a circular dance, at given intervals, and quite in unison, carrying the knives close to their bodies, and wielding them with rapid motion, without actually stabbing themselves.

A loud round of applause greeted this effort. The next item was a similar exhibition, but with curved swords, and to six-eight time. The gambols were all thoroughly in unison, and the men seemed to be attempting to hack off their hands. One or two were actually wounded, and they dropped out, being disqualified from taking any further part in the Kalifa.

The number gradually diminished, and only seven were left when two swords each were served out. Then the actors slashed away, seemingly, in the most reckless manner, dancing all the time. The sword points were placed into their eyes and ears, and the edges round their throats, but not a scratch was sustained. This performance gained the loudest plaudits from the audience. Some pretty Eastern dances were given by Malay women; and the men went through the wonderful fire-dance. The intervals were pleasantly enlivened by the band of the Royal Enniskillen Fusiliers.

Sport under the cloud of apartheid

uring the years of apartheid, the National Party government exploited ignorance and the use of brute force to limit interaction between white and non-white sportsmen. They nurtured a general misconception within the white community that non-whites weren't being seen playing sport because there was a total lack of interest in that particular community towards sport. Officials attributed the under-representation of black sports players to 'deficiencies in temperament'.

The Good Hopes Rugby Team, 1902

White municipal authorities literally 'caged' non-white spectators at international sporting events. Johannesburg corralled them in a wire-netting compound while Cape Town confined them to a space under the trees at the Newlands sports stadium. Such was the degree of non-white 'invisibility' in sporting activities in the 1950s and 1960s that even after the National Party began retreating from the doctrines of apartheid, many white people still believed modern sport to be alien to black and coloured cultures.

This, naturally, was not the case. Gassan Emeran, former principal of Trafalgar High School, based in District Six, recalls: 'Whenever you met people [of colour], it was just rugby – there was nothing else. It was just rugby, rugby, rugby! That was their life. Rugby.'

Although apartheid legislation did not prevent people within the Bo-Kaap from organising or playing sport, the lack of facilities was a major impediment. What passed, in the area, as a rugby ground or cricket pitch was generally an uneven, unfenced, stone-strewn patch of ground – dusty in summer and muddy in winter – with no toilets or changing facilities, and no shelter for spectators.

Thus, as a direct result of the racially segregated South African society at the height of apartheid, non-racial sports organisations were established to try to reunite the non-white ranks of players on the sports field. It is ironic that these non-racial bodies found they were, by the very nature of society at the time, composed of race- based units.

RACISM FORCES 'NON-RACIAL' TO BECOME 'RACIAL'

Take cricket as an example: in 1959, African, coloured, Indian and Malay sectors in the Western Province formed the non-racial Western Province Cricket Board. At the time, the all-white Western Province Cricket Union had an exclusion clause that made it impossible for a non-white player to become a member of that body. Other non-racial provincial boards followed in the footsteps of the first, and in the 1961–62 season, the South African Cricket Board of Control (SACBOC), until then an interracial board but with national units for coloureds, Africans, Indians and Malays as members, changed its constitution to become a reorganised body composed of non-racial provincial units.

When Basil D'Oliveira (classified by the government as 'Cape coloured') moved to England to play for the Middleton Cricket Club in April 1960, the eyes of the world were focused on the state of racial divide within South African sport. Before he arrived in England, D'Oliveira's amazing exploits in matches organised by the non-racial SACBOC had gone completely unnoticed – despite the fact that he'd belted out 50 centuries, including a knock of 225 runs in 70 minutes!

By 1966, D'Oliveira had become a British citizen and had made his Test debut against the West Indies in the second Test at Lord's. At the time, the BBC commentator for the game enthused, 'This is a fairy-tale moment for cricket. We have someone from the heartland of injustice performing in the heartland of the game.'

Unfortunately for the cricket players of the Bo-Kaap – and non-white players throughout the country – they were still very far from realising their own fairy-tale.

D'Oliveira's selection for the British cricket team, which was to tour South Africa in 1968, brought the racial divide in sport to a head. The then South African prime minister, BJ Vorster, protested at the National Party conference, 'The team is not the team of the MCC [the Marylebone Cricket Club, the main cricket authority in Britain] but the team of the anti-apartheid movement … The matter has passed from the realm of sport to the realm of politics. Leftist and liberal politicians have entered the field of sport.'

Hassan Howa
'Mr Cricket'

Hassan Howa was the eldest of Yusuf and Lelia Howa's 12 children. Yusuf, a prominent member of the South African Indian Congress, was keen to impart to Hassan an understanding of politics within South Africa. After matriculating at Trafalgar High School (District Six), Hassan's main passion was sport, in particular, cricket.

During the 1960s he devoted much of his time to promoting cricket. Hassan spoke out against the social injustice of sport being divided along racial lines and his became a strident voice for equality in all sports throughout South Africa. Within the community he was known as 'Mr Cricket' and was frequently invited to address anti-apartheid meetings.

In the 1970s he became the spokesman for a fearless campaign that galvanised the support of mainly Indian and coloured people against white cricket. This brought about an international ban on the Springboks participating in world-class cricket. In 1977 Hassan helped to form the South African Cricket Board (SACB), which was a breakaway organisation from the South African Cricket Union that supported the needs of non-white players. This led also to the formation of the South African Council on Sports (SACOS), which represented numerous black sporting bodies. Through this Hassan lobbied for South Africa's expulsion from world sports competitions, creating the slogan: 'No normal sports in an abnormal society' (see also page 130).

He believed that in order to establish the game on a non-racial level, junior cricket should be introduced at club level. One of his main goals was the establishment of a successful interschool league, and cricket teams were selected at junior club level for interdistrict and interprovincial tournaments. He also allowed provinces to enter Under 21 teams into the B division of competitions run by the South African Cricket Board of Control (SACOB) so that younger players could challenge the more established players.

Ultimately SACOB was absorbed into the formerly whites-only United Cricket Board of South Africa (UCB), which paved the way for South Africa's readmission into world cricket. Hassan, outspoken and not convinced of the merits of the merger, used the resources available to him to provide better sports facilities in underprivileged areas. His special interest was the development of talent, and he helped to identify many young cricketers of colour who could be properly coached to ensure their selection into provincial and national teams; his legacy lives on in the Bo-Kaap today.

Hassan was a member of the committee that received money to bail out students arrested during the 1976 and 1981 riots, and he helped obtain legal representation for these students. He was also a founder member of the United Democratic Front (UDF).

His death in 1992 marked the end of an era for a man who had constantly and fearlessly fought against the evils of racial division in sport. He was survived by his wife, nine children and 12 grandchildren. In 1998 he was posthumously awarded the Presidential Medal.

THE WORLD UNITES IN PROTEST

One month after the original British tour party was selected, the MCC called off the tour because D'Oliveira was not welcome in South Africa. Sport was seen to triumph over the racist politics of apartheid. And as a direct result of this, the International Olympics Committee (IOC) banned South Africa's participation in the 1968 Mexico Olympics. In 1970, the country was expelled from the Olympic Movement and by 1971 South Africa was banned from competition in international cricket.

Throughout this period, SACBOC continued to organise cricket on a non-racial basis up to 1976. The cricket season of 1976–77, however, was one of complete confusion. At the time, secondary schoolchildren marched through Soweto in massive protest against the compulsory use of Afrikaans in schools; hundreds were killed in the violent aftermath. The unrest spread to the Western Cape.

In the sporting arena, things were going from bad to worse for South Africa. On an international level, 21 countries boycotted the Montreal Olympics in protest against New Zealand's rugby team touring South Africa. It was becoming clear that any country having sporting links with South Africa ran the risk of international isolation.

The following year, in October 1977, the South African Cricket Board (SACB) was established (see Fact File, Hassan Howa – 'Mr Cricket' page 128). To the board, non-racialism in sport could only exist in a non-racial society – and which was patently not the case in South Africa. Later that year, the General Assembly of the United Nations passed the International Declaration Against Apartheid in Sport, which called on all member countries to stop sporting contact with South Africa.

When PW Botha became executive state president of South Africa in 1978, it was not surprising that sport reform was to be part of his 'Total Strategy'. Thus, despite the apartheid laws, mixed teams comprising white and non-white players were now permitted to tour. However, this so-called 'normalisation' did not soften the international boycott, because the regime of apartheid remained in force.

A non-racial cricket team under the shadow of apartheid

THE WIND OF CHANGE

In June 1979, the South African Cricket Board, by then affiliated to the South African Council on Sport (SACOS), prepared and submitted a memorandum to the International Cricket Conference. In this document, it laid out the requirements for non-racial sport, implying that none of the restrictions embodied in the Group Areas Act should be allowed to hamper sportsmen or those who administered the game. The following points were made:

(a)   *All clubs must have open membership. Where exclusion clauses are incorporated in club constitutions, these must be removed.*

(b)   *All clubs must participate in competitions organised by single non-racial controlling bodies at local, regional or provincial levels.*

(c)   *A single national non-racial body must control the sport nationally and represent the country internationally.*

(d)   *All sportsmen and sportswomen must have equal opportunities in private and public life.*

(e)   *Sponsorship must be utilised in such a way that all sportsmen benefit equally.*

(f)   *There must be no restrictions placed on clubs or other sports organisations in the acquisition of private sports grounds and club facilities, and all such facilities must be open.*

(g)   *Sports facilities must be provided to all sportsmen without discrimination and on an equal basis.*

(h)   *Selection must be based solely on merit in the composition of representative teams.*

(i)   *South Africa must be represented internationally by a single team selected on merit.*

(j)   *All schoolchildren must be free to attend the schools of their choice and school sports must be free from any restrictions based on race or other abnormal considerations.*

In the 1980s a number of international tours went ahead successfully. British and French rugby teams played again in South Africa in 1980, and the South African rugby team went on tour to South America. At an unofficial level, cricket tours also resumed in South Africa. Fifteen English cricketers, purported to have been paid £50,000 each, arrived in South Africa in 1982 to play a series of games, but this resulted in their suspension from Test cricket in the UK for three years. Throughout the decade an uneasy tension existed in sport, which was not going to go away until apartheid had been resoundingly dismantled.

The unbanning of the African National Congress in the early 1990s paved the way for the formation of single national non-racial sports bodies – and the reintroduction of South Africa into the international sporting fold.

On 24 June 2005, Zahier Ryland, known as 'Kakkerlakkie' ('little cockroach'), became the first person born and raised in the Bo-Kaap to represent the unified Western Province rugby team in the Currie Cup. He made his debut playing left wing against the Cheetahs in Bloemfontein. Zahier's father, Yusuf, had been an outstanding wing for the non-racial Western Province side in the 1970s. Integration into a unified side was no easy transition, however.

Since the end of apartheid there has been much progress, and sport in the Bo-Kaap thrives today. Some would say, however, that change is not fast enough; there still remains a lack of funding and proper facilities within the area.

'FLUFFY' SOLOMONS – SPORTING LEGEND OF THE BO-KAAP

Faghmie Solomons was born in 1957 at 21 Dorp Street in the Bo-Kaap. Due to his family's passion for sport, his interest developed from an early age. His father, who was a member of the Caledonian Roses rugby club in District Six, used to take him and his younger brother along to watch the games. At the time, the main rugby clubs in the Bo-Kaap were the Young Stars, Leeuwendals and Tricolours. They all used the Green Point track, next to the Metropolitan Golf Club, as their training ground. The clubs have since merged to form Schotsche Kloof Rugby Football Club, which is currently the only club in the Bo-Kaap.

During Faghmie's childhood, there were no sports-grounds in the Bo-Kaap for the children to play on, and money was tight, so he emulated his sporting heroes by stuffing old newspapers into an old sock to form a rugby ball. With this he played touch rugby with the other kids on the cobbled road of Dorp Street. He soon gained the nickname, 'Fluffy', because no one could catch him.

At age seven, when he was in Schotsche Kloof Primary School, he started playing for the Callies junior team. He proved to be an all-rounder in the rugby, cricket and soccer teams. In accordance with apartheid law, the schoolchildren were only permitted to play against other non-white schools, and that year his team won the Primary Schools Tournament, with Faghmie playing flank forward. By the age of 13 he was captain of the school's under-65-kilogram rugby squad. He also went on to captain the under-75-kilogram and under-85-kilogram squads.

In those years, annual 'Rag' games were played between the Callies and the Stars at the Green Point track in the first week of October – the last game of the season. While playing for the Stars team, Faghmie was spotted, and later selected as captain of Western Province Primary (coloured) Schools. He was still only 13. With him playing flank forward, the team won the Primary Schools Tournament that year. He was also, during this time, number-four batsman for the Ottomans Juniors Cricket Club in the Bo-Kaap.

Faghmie excelled in cricket. He was selected for the non-racial Western Province Board's Under-19 cricket team in 1972, which played a tournament in Durban. Then, in 1977/78 his selection for the Western Province B side to play a tournament in Kimberley saw him as the tournament's top scorer. He moved into the Western Province A side, which he represented until 1985, playing with cricketers such as 'Leftie' Adams and Salie Masjied.

Morné du Plessis with Faghmie Solomons

Concurrent with his cricket achievements, Faghmie started playing rugby at a more serious level. In 1980 he was nominated captain of the Western Province (non-racial) Rugby Union team, which led ultimately to his becoming captain of the South African Rugby Union side in 1987. He remained captain for two years, during which time the team won numerous trophies, before retiring from the game.

In 2005 Faghmie Solomons and François Pienaar, captain of the 1995 South African rugby side that won the Rugby World Cup Championship, were given honorary awards for dedicated service to South African rugby.

'Fluffy' Solomons in action

Muslim media
A means of cultural and religious exchange

As with any community, a strong sense of identity can be maintained via the media, including print and local radio stations. Besides 'word of mouth' in the community, this is the best way to keep people informed of current debates, religious dialogue, community news and upcoming events. Two major Muslim newspapers and radio stations have serviced the Bo-Kaap over the years.

Farid Sayed has had an intimate working relationship with both newspapers and one of the radio stations. In 1975 Sayed joined the *Muslim News* as a junior reporter; he went on to become the first chairperson of the Western Cape branch of the Union of Black Journalists until it was banned in 1977. He subsequently became an executive member of the provincial branch of the Writers' Association of South Africa. In 1986 he established *Muslim Views*, with himself as founding editor. Both newspapers focus on giving Muslims a written platform, and provide scholarly debate on a wide range of topics. Mahmood Sanglay joined *Muslim Views* in 1997 and is currently the paper's managing editor.

For many years, the only radio stations allowed in South Africa were those that had been sanctioned by the apartheid government. With the dawn of the 1990s and the easing of the grip of media censorship, the concept of local radio stations aimed at the Cape Muslim community seemed at last to be within reach. At this time two main community-based radio stations developed.

Radio 786 was born out of the initial endeavour for unity amongst the country's almost two million Muslims. The Muslim Unity Society, comprising prominent Muslim businessmen in Cape Town, formed the Islamic Unity Convention in March 1994 at a caucus attended by representatives of over 254 Muslim organisations countrywide. The launch of Radio 786 also honoured those members of the Muslim community who had played a significant role in the struggle for liberation against the apartheid regime, the most notable being Imam Abdullah Haron, who was murdered in detention at the hands of security police in 1969. At the launch in September 1995, a 30 000-strong crowd commemorated this event. Radio 786 broadcasts on 100.4 FM stereo in the greater Cape Town area. *Muslim Views* editor Farid Sayed became radio station manager in December 2001.

Voice of the Cape (VOC) developed parallel to Radio 786. It drew its inspiration from respected community *imams*, including Noor Davids and Gasan Solomon, and on the technical and academic acumen of experts such as Anwah Ismail, Moegsien Khan and Dr Achmat Davids. The VOC was granted a special event licence during *Ramadan* in 1995, and subsequent temporary broadcast licences were then granted, permitting the station to broadcast for 24 hours a day, sharing the frequency with Radio 786. In June 2002, VOC was awarded a four-year licence. VOC broadcasts on 100.4 FM from Tygerberg and on 95.8 FM from Paarl and Worcester. The role of these two radio stations is to inform and educate the community about Islam, with a focus on religious teachings, and to report on matters of cultural and political significance.

DIRECTORY OF USEFUL CONTACTS IN THE BO-KAAP

Animals
Bo-Kaap Farm
André
Tel: 021 424 2610
Bird World
Zunaid Suji
Tel: 021 423 9624

Arts and Culture
Actor
Faruk Vally Omar
Tel: 021 423 5901
Blank Projects
(contemporary gallery)
Jonathan Garnham
Wed 16:00–19:00
by appointment
198 Buitengracht Street
Cell: 072 198 9221
Delos
(chandeliers and antiques)
Jerome
140 Buitengracht Street
Tel: 021 424 7573
Cell: 082 563 6616
Jewel Africa
170 Buitengracht Street
Tel: 021 424 5141
Make-up artist
Salma Misbach
Tel: 021 424 0529
Cell: 072 236 3009
Maxi's Jewellery Merchants
15 Jordaan Street,
Schotsche Kloof
Tel: 021 426 2652
Mieda Embroidery Art
Tel: 021 423 0208

Monkeybiz
(bead artists)
43 Rose Street
Tel: 021 426 0145
Painting on canvas
Ishmael Achmat
Tel: 021 424 4862
Cell: 082 710 0230
Pottery Art
Vasanti Jaga
Tel: 021 424 3858
Soni Art Studios
(Islamic calligraphy)
3 Soni Road
Crawford
Tel: 021 697 3941
Street Wires
(wire art)
77 Shortmarket Street
Tel: 021 426 2475
Sunshine Entertainers
(traditional performers)
Rashaad Ajam
Tel: 021 426 1425
Xcon Films
Munir Parker
Tel: 021 424 1848
Cell: 083 419 0558

Associations
Bo-Kaap Civic Association
Mogammad
Tel: 021 426 2915
Cell: 073 826 4959
Bo-Kaap Senior Citizens Club
Yasmiena Salie
Tel: 021 423 7574

Malaysian Historical Society
Ismail Petersen
Tel: 021 593 6816

Building and related services
Abrach Building Contractors
Rushdie
Tel: 021 447 7869
Cell: 076 987 1975
Carpets and laminated flooring
Y Johaar
Tel: 021 423 6916
Electrician
Nazeem Wiener
Tel: 021 422 2088
Flooring specialist
Cassiem Allie
Tel: 021 423 2777
or 021 638 7060
I.D. Installation
Mailie
Tel: 021 424 5577
Cell: 083 525 5339
Jardeen Building Contractors
Tel: 021 422 3478
Cell: 073 515 9122
Pro-Clean Carpets
Siraaj Habib
Cell: 076 051 6540
Professional Tiler
Sulayman Fakier
Tel: 021 426 1806

Dressmakers and designers
AB Dress Designs
Mr Salie
Tel: 021 423 3466
or 021 424 4221

Dressmaker
Fatima
Tel: 021 426 5147
Dressmaker
Miriam
Tel: 021 424 1395

Food and catering
Atlas Trading Co.
(dried fruit and spices)
94 Wale Street
Tel: 021 423 4361
**Cooking experience
for tourists**
(homebased)
Tel: 021 423 9978
Dollie's Homebakes
Tel: 021 424 8515
Flava 2 Savour Caterers
Sumaiya
Tel: 021 422 3496
Cell: 083 660 8253
Koeksister specialist
Hati Davids
Tel: 021 424 6752
Koeksister specialist
Miriam Adams
Tel: 021 423 3509
Malay Fast Food
Anēsa
Tel: 021 422 1847
or 021 424 4571
Naz's Kitchen
Nazlie
Tel: 021 424 5577
Shaheda Caterers
Tel: 021 426 4514
Cell: 082 597 9587
S Wagiet Caterers
Tel: 021 424 9736
Cell: 082 084 7347

Tea/lunch/dinner at home
Gabebah Jassiem
Tel: 021 424 7717
Cell: 084 310 7865

Miscellaneous
Legacy Estates
(property agent)
Ilyas Salie
Tel: 021 426 5962
Hiring Services
(crockery and cutlery)
Sulayman Soeker
Tel: 021 510 1296

Museums and attractions
Bo-Kaap Museum
(Iziko Museums)
71 Wale Street
Tel: 021 481 3939
District Six Museum
25A Buitenkant Street
Tel: 021 466 7200
Noon Gun British Battery
Dudley
Tel: 021 469 1257
The Slave Lodge
cnr Adderley and Wale streets
Tel: 021 460 8242

Religious Activities
Free lectures
Dr Mogamat Faadiel Arnold
Tel: 021 424 3921
Introduction to psychology
and methodology of the
Holy Qur'an
Thursday nights, 20:00
at Darul Huda Hall, Bryant Street
Dr Salie Adams
Recital of the Holy Qur'an
Monday nights, 20:00
at Darul Huda Hall, Bryant Street

Sheikh Siraaj Johaar
Tel: 021 797 6543
Hadj classes:
Thursday nights, 20:00
Youth programmes:
Monday nights, 20:00
Nurul Islam Mosque
Buitengracht Street

Restaurants and cafés
African Café
Tel: 021 422 0482
Allie's Corner Shop
160 Strand Street
Tel: 021 419 1253
Biesmiellah Restaurant
(Malay cuisine)
2 Upper Wale Street
Tel: 021 423 0850
Bo-Kaap Kombuis
(Malay cuisine)
7 August Street
Tel: 021 422 5446
Home-based restaurant,
3 Morris Street
Tel: 021 424 0719
Marco's African Place
(African cuisine)
15 Rose Street
Tel: 021 423 5412
**Noon Gun Restaurant
and Tea Room**
(Malay cuisine)
273 Longmarket Street
Tel: 021 424 0529
Rose Corner Café
100 Wale Street
Tel: 021 424 2660

Shoes, leather goods and repairs
Rocksole Shoes and Bags
61–63 Wale Street
Tel: 021 424 3858

Tour guides

Bo-Kaap Guided Tours
  Shireen Narkedien
  (registered guide)
  Tel: 021 422 1554
  Cell: 082 423 6932

Cape Heritage Tours
  Bilqees Baker
  (registered guide)
  Tel: 021 424 3736
  Cell: 083 364 7514

Crescent Tours
  Fasiegh
  Cell: 072 368 8542
  Cassiem
  Cell: 082 786 1304
  crescentours@gmail.com
  www.crescentours.com

Tana Baru Tours
  Shereen Misbach Habib
  (registered guide)
  Tel: 021 424 0719
  Cell: 073 237 3800

Tourist accommodation

Alawia Allie Home-Stay
  Tel: 021 423 2777
  Cell: 082 926 5972

August Street Guest House and B&B
  Yusuf Larney
  Tel: 021 422 5446
  Cell: 082 421 9508

Bo-Kaap Village Lodge B&B
  Fauldaine Ishmael
  Chiappini Street
  Tel: 021 424 7860
  Cell: 083 448 9828
  surabi@telkomsa.net
  www.tiscover.co.za/bo-kaap

Ella Street Guest House
  Amien Jakoet
  Tel: 021 424 0803
  Cell: 083 457 9725

Fatgiah's Home-Stay
  Tel: 021 426 1806
  Cell: 073 316 2938

Shereen Misbach Habib
  Tel: 021 424 0719

Signal Hill Lodge B&B
  Tel: 021 426 5363

View-T-Full Guest House and B&B
  (self-catering)
  Ighsaan Moosa
  Tel: 021 423 2516
  Cell: 083 257 6471

Zainab's Home-Stay
  Tel: 021 424 0719
  Cell: 082 096 0107

Tourist information

Cape Town Tourism
  Burg Street
  Tel: 021 426 4260

Travel agencies

Latiefah Travel & Tours
  145 Schotsche Kloof Flats
  Astana Street
  Tel: 021 424 5512

BIBLIOGRAPHY

~ Booth, Douglas and Nauright, John, 'Embodied Identities: Sport and Race in South Africa', *Paper in Contours – A Journal of the African Diaspora* (Spring 2003). Vol. 1 No. 1

~ Constant-Martin, Denis, *Coon Carnival, New Year in Cape Town, Past and Present* (1999). David Philip Publishers

~ Da Costa, Yusuf, and Davids, Achmat, *Pages from Cape Muslim History* (1st Ed 1994). Shuter & Shooter

~ D'Arcy, Dr MC, 'The Evolutionary Art of Achmat Soni', *Muslim Views*, November 2002

~ Davids, Achmat, *The Mosques of Bo-Kaap – A Social History of Islam at the Cape* (1st Ed 1980). The South African Institute of Arabic and Islamic Research, Athlone

~ Davids, Achmat, *The History of the Tana Baru* (1st Ed 1985). The Committee for the Preservation of the Tana Baru

~ Du Plessis, Dr ID, 'The Malay Quarter' (1972). *Standard Encyclopaedia of Southern Africa*, Nasou Limited

~ Jacobs, R, *The Slave Book* (1999). Kwela Publishers

~ Jaffer, Mansoor (Ed.), *Guide to the Kramats of the Western Cape* (2nd Impression 2001). Cape Mazaar (Kramat) Society

~ Johannesson, Barbara, *The Cape of Slaves – Slavery in the Cape Colony 1658–1838* (1st Ed 1995). Sached Books, Heinemann Publishers

~ Khalifa, Dr R, *Mathematical Miracle of the Quran*, An Appendix in the English Translation of the Qur'an

~ Mountain, Alan, *An Unsung Heritage – Perspectives on Slavery* (1st Ed 2004). David Philip Publishers

~ Musee d'art et d'histoire (1988). *Islamic Calligraphy:* Sacred and Secular Writings, Catalog of the exhibition held at the Musee d'art et d'histoire, Geneva and other locations 1988–1989

~ Ross, Robert, *Cape of Torments – Slavery and Resistance in South Africa* (1st Ed 1983). Routledge & Kegan Paul Publishers (International Library of Anthropology)

~ Van Heyningen, Dr Elizabeth (Ed.), *Studies in the History of Cape Town, Cape Town History Project* (1st Ed 1994). UCT Press (Pty) Ltd in association with the Centre for African Studies